200

TH ~~~~ **TES**

D1440348

An Hachette UK Company
www.hachette.co.uk

First published in Great Britain in 2009 by Hamlyn,
a division of Octopus Publishing Group Ltd,
Carmelite House, 50 Victoria Embankment,
London EC4Y 0DZ
www.octopusbooks.co.uk

This edition published in 2016

ISBN 978-0-600-63346-4

A CIP catalogue record for this book is available
from the British Library

Printed and bound in China

10 9 8 7 6 5 4 3 2 1

Standard level spoon measurement are used in all recipes.
1 tablespoon = one 15 ml spoon
1 teaspoon = one 5 ml spoon

Both imperial and metric measures have been given in all
recipes. Use one set of measurements only and not a mixture
of both.

Eggs should be medium unless otherwise stated. The
Department of Health advises that eggs should not be
consumed raw. This book contains dishes made with raw or
lightly cooked eggs. It is prudent for more vulnerable people
such as pregnant and nursing mothers, invalids, the elderly,
babies and young children to avoid uncooked or lightly
cooked dishes made with eggs. Once prepared these dishes
should be kept refrigerated and used promptly.

Ovens should be preheated to the specific temperature – if
using a fan-assisted oven, follow the manufacturer's
instructions for adjusting the time and the temperature.

This book includes dishes made with nuts and nut
derivatives. It is advisable for customers with known allergic
reactions to nuts and nut derivatives and those who may be
potentially vulnerable to these allergies, such as pregnant and
nursing mothers, invalids, the elderly, babies and children, to
avoid dishes made with nuts and nut oils. It is also prudent to
check the labels of pre-prepared ingredients for the possible
inclusion of nut derivatives.

contents

introduction

introduction

My purpose in writing this book is to show you, in as compact a form as possible, how to prepare a wide selection of popular Thai dishes, adding to each recipe at least one variation using slightly different ingredients. Because the book is so condensed, I have described in the introduction some of the ingredients you may not be familiar with, as well as some basic procedures and recipes.

Whenever I go back to Thailand, I'm always impressed by the high standard of cooking, not only in restaurants but also from the stalls in the many street markets you find all over Bangkok and other cities (and even along the major trunk roads). So-called 'street food' deserves a better name, because it bears little resemblance to its equivalent in the West. Wealthy people send out their maids to buy cooked food from the local market, knowing that it will have been prepared by someone who specializes in that particular dish, often bringing it to perfection. Thai people are justly proud of their cuisine and I am very happy to explain some of its secrets.

developing taste

I gained my knowledge of Thai cooking partly from my family, partly from helping people who are masters of their art, and partly from my own experiments. All of this practical activity has been valuable, yet probably the most important part has been the entirely passive role of eating Thai food and developing good judgement about it. Maybe, too, there's a Buddhist element to this process – coming from the monks who tell us to concentrate while we eat, to think about what we are doing, instead of munching away while talking about something else. Thai people rarely eat in silence, but the conversation nearly always turns to the food in front of us. We discuss it avidly. 'Lovely, but a bit too salty…', 'Almost perfect, but maybe a bit more tamarind…', and so on. If you eat enough Thai food, especially with Thai friends, you'll soon develop your palate.

from the beginning

If you're a complete beginner who has never cooked – or even tasted – Thai food, don't worry. This book describes the preparation and cooking step by step, using precise

measurements. In practice, Thai cooks are not inclined to be very precise about measurement, preferring to rely on their experience. For this reason, I have had to recreate the dishes rather than merely translate them from existing Thai recipes.

main characteristics

Like a particular style of music, Thai food is instantly recognizable because dishes have certain characteristics in common. We are fond of using fresh herbs like lemon grass, galangal, ginger, coriander and kaffir lime leaves. We like the tasty parts of plants that grow below ground, like some of those just mentioned, plus shallots, garlic and others. Thai cuisine is the only one in the world to use the roots of the coriander plant as well as its stalks and leaves. We are quite economical in our use of ingredients – nothing is thrown away that can be saved for another dish.

Apart from its distinctive range of ingredients, the other main characteristic of Thai food is the way in which we prepare it. For example, we like to cut meat into very thin slices so that it cooks quickly. Thai food tends to take quite a long time to prepare, but the cooking is usually quick and easy. For this reason, it's ideal if you're having a dinner party because you can prepare the food an hour or two in advance, then cook and serve the meal right on time.

equipment

You don't need much special equipment for cooking Thai food. Standard saucepans, plates and bowls can be found in most people's kitchens. I should, however, mention a few really useful items:

Nonstick wok – this is a good investment if you plan to cook oriental food frequently; choose a size suitable for the number of people you plan to serve.

Nonstick saucepans and frying pans are vital; always have at least one small pan for preparing sauces.

Very sharp knife – this is the most useful tool in the kitchen.

Rolling pin and pastry board

Steamer – you can use either a traditional, standard steamer rack or a bamboo basket steamer.

Blender or mixer – or a pestle and mortar if you want to crush herbs more finely.

for the cupboard

You'll need a few standard ingredients in your storecupboard that are not normally used in Western cooking.

bamboo shoots

A few small cans of sliced bamboo shoots are a good standby to add to curries and other main dishes.

coconut milk

A key ingredient of many Thai curries and other dishes, coconut milk is a rich, creamy liquid derived from the flesh of a coconut.

fish sauce

There are many types of oriental fish sauce, made from different species of fish, such as anchovies.

oyster sauce

This is made by boiling oysters in water to make a white broth, then condensing it to a dark brown sauce.

mung bean vermicelli (*wun sen*)

Sometimes also called 'transparent noodles', 'cellophane noodles' or 'glass noodles'. They become transparent when cooked.

rice noodles (small)

In dried form, rice noodles are a standard storecupboard ingredient. Dried *(sen lek)* noodles are about 2.5 mm (⅛ inch) wide; the

flat (*sen yai*) type are 1–2.5 cm (½–1 inch) wide. Rice vermicelli noodles (*sen mee*) are very thin indeed. Soak or cook noodles in boiling water according to the packet instructions. Drain, then add to a bowl of water until they cool down, drain again and use as required.

sesame oil

A lovely dark amber oil that's very aromatic. It's used as a flavouring rather than for frying.

soy sauce (light)

Made from soybeans or mushrooms, light soy sauce is a thin, opaque, brown liquid, lighter in colour than some kinds. It adds saltiness to the dish without affecting its colour.

water chestnuts

The crispy white flesh of small, round water-chestnut corms adds a crunchy texture to some dishes. Buy them in cans.

for the freezer

The only key ingredients that have to be kept deep frozen are spring roll sheets

(12 cm/5 inch square) and wonton sheets. Defrost them before use. You can also put leftover fresh lemon grass, galangal, kaffir lime leaves or even coconut milk (in tightly sealed and dated bags) into a freezer where they will keep for 2 or 3 months.

other selected ingredients

These are a few of the most typical, possibly unfamiliar ingredients.

chillies

The two main types of chilli used in Thai cooking are small, fresh, 'bird's-eye' chillies (a distinctive variety about 2.5–5 cm/1–2 inches long, grown in Thailand), and fresh or dried red chillies that are much larger (about 12 cm/5 inches long) and not nearly as hot, but they add a lovely mellow flavour to your dishes. Fresh chillies may be green or red, the red (ripe) ones being more frequently used.

coriander

Much enjoyed in the West, but usually sold without any roots. Try to find some with a little bit of root if the recipe calls for it, although stalk is a good alternative. We use ground coriander too. The fresh leaves are frequently used as a garnish.

dried fungus

You can buy both dried black and white fungus from most Asian grocers. Soak in hot water for 2–3 minutes and drain before using.

galangal

A key ingredient of Thai curry paste, galangal looks like ginger but tastes very different. It's hard to slice, so be careful.

goji (wolf) berries

I have always used sun-dried Tibetan goji berries in my cooking, as many Thais do. They are now regarded as a 'superfood', being exceptionally rich in antioxidants.

kaffir lime leaves

The only ingredient listed here that may be difficult to obtain in the West. They are used for adding flavour to curries.

lemon grass

Another key ingredient of Thai curry paste, lemon grass adds a delicate lemon flavour to many dishes. You can finely slice lemon grass and add it directly to food that is to be well cooked. Alternatively, bruise thick stalks for cooking and later removal. Buy fresh stalks that are not too dry.

limes
We prefer to use limes rather than lemons, but you can substitute lemon if necessary.

soya protein mince
This is made from soya beans and has a chewy consistancy similar to meat. It is high in protein, fibre and iron and completely free from from cholesterol and fat.

tamarind
Made from the dried pulp of tamarind seeds, this can be purchased in tubs as a paste. It adds tartness to sweet and sour sauces. To make a tamarind purée you mix bought dried tamarind pulp with boiling water (see page 90).

taro
A white root vegetable. The starchy corm of the broad-leaved taro plant is not unlike sweet potato in texture, and it needs cooking until tender.

thai aubergines
Quite unlike the purple variety, Thai aubergines have a bitter flavour and come in two sizes: pea and golf-ball.

thai sweet basil leaves
These are distinctive both for their purple stems and for their aniseed flavour.

spices
Although we like to use fresh herbs wherever possible, occasionally we use spice powders, especially in dishes from the south of Thailand where there's a strong Malaysian influence. We like to add a little spice to Thai curry paste. I've already mentioned ground coriander (strictly speaking, a herb). Other useful powders in Thai cooking include: ground cumin, ground white pepper, ground allspice, ground turmeric and yellow curry powder.

how to prepare seafood

crabs
Place them in the freezer for an hour. Then, leaving the legs attached, cut them in half through the centre of the shell from head to rear. Repeat this procedure from left to right, quartering the crab. Twist off the legs and remove the upper shell pieces. Discard the stomach sac and soft gill tissue. Use crackers or the back of a heavy knife to crack the crab claws and make them easier to eat.

mussels

You can buy mussels without shells, either fresh or frozen.

prawns

Peel, de-vein and cut each raw prawn open along the back so it opens out like a butterfly. Leave each prawn joined along the base and at the tail.

scallops

Slice off and discard any veins, membrane or hard white muscle from each scallop. Small scallops can be left whole, but you can cut the larger ones in half.

squid

Peel off the outer skin of the squid and rinse out the insides of the tubes. Cut each in half and open the pieces out. Score the inside of each squid with diagonal cuts to make a diamond pattern, then cut them into squares.

useful tips

deep-frying

If the recipe calls for deep-frying, it's vital to know exactly how hot to have the oil in the wok or large frying pan. Heat the oil over a medium heat, but not so hot that it spits out. You can test it with the food you're frying. Drop in a small piece, and the oil will be hot enough if the piece sizzles immediately.

no blender?

If you don't have a blender, you can finely chop ingredients such as garlic or coriander roots by hand. Keep chopping and the result will be much the same.

adjusting the seasoning

Nearly every dish in this book requires the cook to 'taste and adjust the seasoning'. In the ingredients list you'll see various condiments or flavourings listed, such as lime juice, fish sauce, light soy sauce, sea salt or ground black pepper. Add most of the quantity stated, but retain a little bit to add more flavour if you think the dish requires it. This is standard practice for all Thai cooking.

make a start

If you use the right ingredients and follow the recipes closely, there's no reason why you should not create a lovely Thai meal with your very first attempt. Happy cooking!

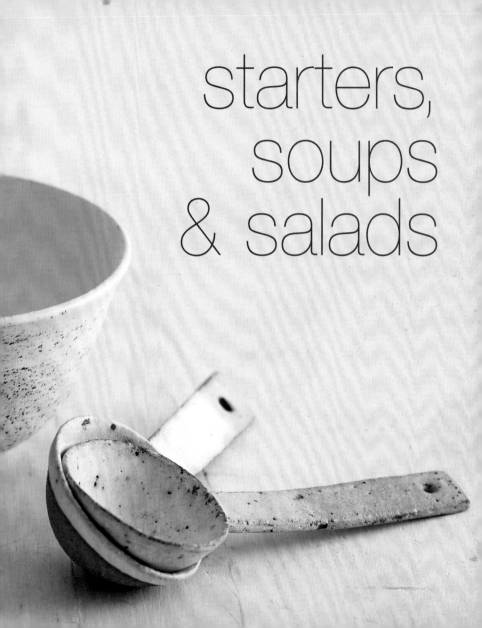

starters, soups & salads

gold bags

Makes **40**
Preparation time **40 minutes**
Cooking time **40 minutes**

1½ tablespoons **plain flour**
6 tablespoons **cold water**
60 long **chives**
425 g (14 oz) **minced raw
    prawns**
150 g (5 oz) can **water
    chestnuts**, drained and
    roughly chopped
3–4 **garlic cloves**, finely
    chopped
¼ teaspoon **ground white
    pepper**
½ teaspoon **salt**
200 g (7 oz) pack (about 50)
    frozen **spring roll sheets**,
    12 cm (5 inches) square,
    defrosted
sunflower oil, for deep-frying

Mix the flour and water in a saucepan until smooth. Stir over a medium heat for 2–3 minutes or until thick, and set aside.

Finely chop 10 of the chives. Mix the prawns, water chestnuts, garlic, chopped chives, pepper and salt.

Clean and soak the remaining chives in hot water for 2 minutes until soft, then drain and dry.

Spoon 1 teaspoon of filling into the middle of a spring roll sheet. Use your finger to brush around it with flour paste, pull up the 4 corners and pinch together, enclosing the filling. Tie with a chive and lay on a tray. Repeat until finished.

Heat 7 cm (3 inches) of oil in a wok over a medium heat. The oil is ready when a small piece of spring roll sheet sizzles when dropped in. Deep-fry batches of 10 bags for 8–10 minutes until lightly browned and crispy. Drain on kitchen paper. Serve hot or warm, with Sweet Chilli Sauce (see page 36).

For gold purses, replace the spring roll sheets with 50 wonton sheets, 7 cm (3 inches) square, defrosted if frozen. Omit the flour, water and most of the chives, retaining about 5. Use half the ingredients plus 1 tablespoon oyster sauce. After mixing the ingredients, place about ½ teaspoon into the middle of each sheet. Brush the edges with water and gather up, squeezing the corners together to make a purse. Deep-fry each batch for 4–5 minutes until crispy.

sesame prawn toast

Makes **10–12 pieces**
Preparation time **20 minutes**
Cooking time **20 minutes**

3–4 **garlic cloves**, roughly
    chopped
2–3 **coriander roots** and
    stalks, roughly chopped
300 g (10 oz) **minced raw**
    prawns
¼ teaspoon **ground white**
    pepper
⅓ teaspoon **sea salt**
1 large **egg**
5–6 slices **white bread**,
    crusts removed, each slice
    cut into 2 triangles, dried
    overnight or grilled for
    1–2 minutes each side
    until dry
5–6 tablespoons **sesame**
    seeds
sunflower oil, for deep-frying

Use a pestle and mortar or a small blender to pound
or blend the garlic and the coriander roots and stalks
into a paste. Add the prawns, pepper, salt and egg and
mix together.

Spread the prawn paste thickly on one side of each
piece of dry bread. Sprinkle with sesame seeds and
press down firmly.

Heat 5 cm (2 inches) of oil in a wok over a medium
heat. The oil is ready when a small piece of bread
sizzles when dropped in. (It is important not to have the
oil too hot or the bread will cook too quickly and turn
brown.) Deep-fry a few pieces at a time, paste-side
down, for 3–4 minutes or until golden brown. Lift out
with a slotted spoon and place them paste side up on
kitchen paper.

Serve hot or warm as a starter with Sweet Chilli Sauce
(see page 36).

For coriander chicken toast, replace the prawns
and sesame seeds with 300 g (10 oz) minced
chicken. Press coriander leaves and chilli slices on
each one and deep-fry for 5–6 minutes, following the
method as above.

golden baskets

Makes **30**

Preparation time **30–40 minutes**

Cooking time **15–20 minutes**

4 tablespoons **sunflower oil**

2 **garlic cloves**, finely chopped

200 g (7 oz) **minced chicken** or **prawns**

25 g (1 oz) **carrots**, finely diced

50 g (2 oz) mixed **sweetcorn kernels** and **petits pois**, thawed if frozen

50 g (2 oz) **red pepper**, deseeded, finely diced

1 tablespoon **light soy sauce**

½ teaspoon **ground white pepper**

pinch of **curry powder**

½ teaspoon **caster sugar**

1 **spring onion**, finely chopped

200 g (7 oz) pack **spring roll sheets**, 12 cm (5 inches) square, or **filo pastry**

To garnish

30 **coriander leaves**

a few slices of **red chilli**

Heat 1½ tablespoons of the oil in a wok or large frying pan and stir-fry the garlic over a medium heat until it is lightly browned. Add the chicken or prawns, crumbling and breaking up the meat until it has separated and is cooked through.

Add the carrots, sweetcorn, petits pois and red pepper and stir-fry for 1–2 minutes. Add the soy sauce, pepper, curry powder, sugar and spring onion, combine well and set aside.

Cut the spring roll sheets or filo pastry into 60 squares, each 6 x 6 cm (2½ x 2½ inches). Brushing the sheets with a little oil as you use them, lay 2 squares in each indentation in a small bun tin used for making 3.5 cm (1½ inch) cakes, overlapping the squares so that the top sheet is at an angle of 45 degrees to the bottom one. Prepare 30 baskets and bake in a preheated oven, 180°C (350°F), Gas Mark 4, for 10–12 minutes or until they are crispy and golden brown. Carefully remove the baskets and allow them to cool slightly.

Spoon the filling into the baskets and serve at room temperature, each garnished with a coriander leaf and some slices of chilli.

For vegetarian golden baskets, replace the chicken or prawns with 75 g (3 oz) finely chopped button mushrooms or firm bean curd. Soak in hot water for 6–7 minutes. Add the mushrooms after the garlic has browned and then stir-fry the rest of the ingredients as above. If you are using bean curd add it in before adding the soy sauce.

chicken satay

Makes **40 sticks**
Preparation time **30 minutes**,
  plus marinating
Cooking time **40 minutes**

1 kg (2 lb) skinless **chicken fillets**

Marinade
4–5 **garlic cloves**, roughly
  chopped
4 **coriander roots** and **stalks**,
  roughly chopped
3 **shallots**, roughly chopped
2.5 cm (1 inch) piece of **fresh
  root ginger**, peeled and
  thinly sliced
1 tablespoon **ground
  coriander**
1 tablespoon **ground cumin**
1 tablespoon **ground
  turmeric**
1 teaspoon **curry powder**
400 ml (14 fl oz) can **coconut
  milk**
1½ tablespoons **fish sauce**
50 g (2 oz) **coconut**, palm
  or **brown sugar** or
  4 tablespoons **clear honey**
4 tablespoons **sunflower oil**
1¼ teaspoons **sea salt**

Cut the chicken into slices and put them in a bowl.

Use a pestle and mortar or a small blender to pound
or blend the garlic, coriander roots, shallots and ginger
to a paste. Mix with the chicken, along with rest of
the marinade ingredients. Cover and leave to marinate
in the refrigerator for a minimum of 4 hours, but
preferably overnight.

Thread the chicken pieces on to bamboo skewers
that have been soaked in water for 30 minutes, leaving
some space at either end. Place them under a hot
grill for about 4–5 minutes on each side or until the
chicken is cooked through and very slightly charred.
Turn frequently, brushing the marinade over the meat
during cooking.

Serve hot or warm with chopped raw onion and
chunks of cucumber and a peanut sauce.

For homemade peanut sauce, heat 1½ tablespoons
of oil in a saucepan and stir-fry 1 tablespoon red or
massaman curry paste for 3–4 minutes or until
fragrant. Add 200 ml (7 fl oz) coconut milk, 200 ml
(7 fl oz) vegetable stock, 1½ oz sugar, 1½ tablespoons
light soy sauce, 3 tablespoons tamarind purée (see
page 90) or 1 tablespoon lime juice, 150 g (5 oz)
roughly chopped roasted peanuts and 15 g (½ oz)
dried breadcrumbs and stir together. Taste and adjust
the seasoning, using a little more sugar, light soy
sauce, tamarind purée or lime juice if necessary. If the
sauce is too thick before serving, add a little milk.

spring rolls

Makes **50**
Preparation time **1 hour**
Cooking time **30 minutes**

50 g (2 oz) **mung bean
vermicelli**
½ handful **dried black fungus**
1½ tablespoons **plain flour**
6 tablespoons **water**
1½ tablespoons **sunflower oil**
3–4 **garlic cloves**, finely
chopped
125 g (4 oz) **minced raw
prawns**
50 g (2 oz) **carrots**, finely
shredded
50 g (2 oz) frozen **peas**,
defrosted
50 g (2 oz) frozen **sweetcorn
kernels**, defrosted
150 g (5 oz) **bean sprouts**
1 cm (½ inch) piece of **fresh
root ginger**, peeled, finely
grated
1½ tablespoons **light soy
sauce**
¼ teaspoon **ground white
pepper**
200 g (7 oz) pack **spring roll
sheets**, 12 cm (5 inches)
square
sunflower oil, for deep-frying

Soak the vermicelli in hot water for 4–5 minutes or
until soft. Drain and cut with a sharp knife to shorten
the noodles.

Soak the black fungus in boiling water for
3–4 minutes until soft, then drain. Remove, discard
the hard stalks and finely chop.

Mix the flour and water in a small saucepan until
smooth. Stir and cook over a medium heat for
2–3 minutes or until thick.

Heat 1½ tablespoons of oil in a wok and lightly brown
the garlic. Add the prawns, vermicelli, soaked fungus,
carrots, peas, sweetcorn, bean sprouts, ginger, soy
sauce and pepper and cook for 4–5 minutes. Taste
and adjust the seasoning. Allow to cool.

Place a few spring roll sheets on a work surface.
Spoon 2 teaspoons of the filling along the side nearest
to you. Bring the edge up, then roll it away from you a
half-turn over the filling. Fold the sides into the centre,
then wrap and seal the join tightly with flour paste and
lay on a tray. Repeat with the rest.

Heat 5 cm (2 inches) of oil in a wok over a medium
heat. Deep-fry small batches for 8–10 minutes until
crispy. Drain on kitchen paper. Serve hot or warm, with
Sweet Chilli Sauce (see page 36).

For vegetarian spring rolls, omit the prawns, use
100 g (3½ oz) vermicelli and include an extra 50 g
(2 oz) bean sprouts or finely shredded cabbage. Add
all the ingredients after the garlic has lightly browned
and become fragrant.

thai egg strips

Serves **2**

Preparation time **5 minutes**

Cooking time **1–2 minutes**

3 **eggs**, beaten

1 **shallot**, finely sliced

1 **spring onion**, thinly sliced

1 long **red chilli**, finely
chopped

1 tablespoon chopped
coriander leaves

½ tablespoon **light soy sauce**

⅛ teaspoon **ground white
pepper**

1½ tablespoons **sunflower oil**

spring onion, cut into fine
strips, to garnish (optional)

Mix the eggs, shallot, spring onion, chilli, coriander leaves, light soy sauce and pepper in a bowl.

Heat the oil in a nonstick frying pan or wok, pour in the egg mixture and swirl it around the pan to produce a large, thin omelette. Cook for 1–2 minutes until firm.

Slide the omelette out on to a plate and roll it up as though it were a pancake. Allow to cool.

Cut the cooled omelette roll crossways into 5 mm (¼ inch) or 1 cm (½ inch) sections, depending on how wide you want your strips to be. Serve them still rolled up or straightened out, in a heap, garnished with strips of spring onion, if liked.

For spicy egg with Thai basil leaves, omit the shallot, spring onion, long red chilli and coriander leaves. Mix the eggs with the light soy sauce and pepper. Lightly brown 2 finely chopped garlic cloves in a frying pan, add 2 finely chopped small red chillies and a handful of chopped fresh Thai basil leaves and stir-fry for a minute or so. Add the egg mixture to the pan and brown both sides of the omelette. Serve with rice or as a side dish.

fish cakes

Makes **20–25 (or 8 large)**
Preparation time **20 minutes**
Cooking time **30 minutes**

500 g (1 lb) **minced skinless
fish fillets** (such as
monkfish, cod, haddock,
salmon or mackerel)
1 tablespoon **Red Curry
Paste** (see page 94)
2 tablespoons **self-raising
flour**
½ teaspoon **sea salt**
50 g (2 oz) **green beans**,
finely sliced
3 **kaffir lime leaves**, finely
shredded
1 large **egg**, lightly beaten
sunflower oil, for pan-frying

Mix together the minced fish, curry paste, flour, sea salt,
green beans, kaffir lime leaves and egg in a bowl.

Heat a little oil in a nonstick frying pan. Using your
wet hands or a spoon, shape the fish mixture into
20–25 small, thin, flat cakes, 2.5 cm (1 inch) across,
and gently pan-fry in batches for 4–5 minutes each
side (or 6–8 minutes each side for large fish cakes).
Drain on kitchen paper.

Add a little oil to the pan for each batch. Serve hot or
warm with Sweet Chilli Sauce (see page 36).

For crab cakes, replace the fish with 500 g (1 lb)
cooked crab meat (drain off the liquid if using canned
crab). You can omit the curry paste if you want a mild
taste, but red curry paste will make it spicy (you can
easily make 2 quantities of paste and use one for a red
curry dish and the other for your fish or crab cakes).

green papaya with chilli & lime

Serves **1**

Preparation time **10 minutes**

1 **garlic clove**

25 g (1 oz) **roasted peanuts**

125 g (4 oz) **green papaya**,
   finely shredded

25 g (1 oz) **green beans**, cut
   into 2.5 cm (1 inch) lengths

1 teaspoon **ground dried
   shrimp**

1 small **bird's-eye red chilli**

1 tablespoon **clear honey**

½ tablespoon **fish sauce**

juice and rind of ½ **lime**

2 **cherry tomatoes**

Use a wooden pestle and clay mortar to pound the garlic. Add the peanuts and pound roughly with the garlic. Add the papaya and pound softly, using a spoon to scrape down the sides, turning and mixing well.

Add the green beans and ground shrimp and keep pounding and turning to soften these ingredients. Add the chilli, honey and fish sauce, then add in the lime juice and add the lime rind to the mixture. Lightly pound together for another minute.

Add the tomatoes and lightly pound for another minute. As the juice comes out, pound more gently so the liquid doesn't splash. Taste and adjust the seasoning – it should be a balance of sweet and sour with a hot taste.

Spoon the papaya salad and all the juices on to a serving plate.

For mixed vegetables with chilli & lime, replace the papaya and beans with 150 g (5 oz) carrot and cabbage, finely shredded. Use 1 tablespoon coconut sugar, palm sugar or honey. Vegetarians can omit the ground shrimp and use light soy sauce instead of fish sauce, but the food will become slightly darker as a result.

son-in-law eggs

Serves **4**

Preparation time **10 minutes**

Cooking time **40 minutes**

6 large **eggs**

sunflower oil, for deep-frying

2 **dried red chillies**, about
12 cm (5 inches) long, cut
into 1 cm (½ inch) pieces,
deseeded

125 g (4 oz) **shallots**, finely
sliced

1½–2 tablespoons **fish sauce**

4 tablespoons **Tamarind
Purée** (see page 90) or
2 tablespoons **lime juice**

150 g (5 oz) **coconut, palm**
or **brown sugar**, or 10
tablespoons **clear honey**

Boil the eggs in a saucepan of water, lower the heat
and simmer for 8–10 minutes. Drain, then crack the
shells slightly and cool under cold running water. Peel
off the shells.

Heat about 7 cm (3 inches) of oil in a wok over a
medium heat. The oil is ready when a slice of shallot
sizzles when dropped into it. Deep-fry the chillies
for a few seconds to bring out the flavour. Drain on
kitchen paper.

Deep-fry the shallots for 6–8 minutes until golden
brown and crispy. Remove and drain. Lower each egg
into the same hot oil and deep-fry for 6–10 minutes
or until browned. Remove and drain.

Remove the oil from the wok and add the fish sauce,
tamarind purée or lime juice and sugar and stir for
5–6 minutes or until the sugar has dissolved. Taste
and adjust the seasoning.

Halve the eggs lengthways and arrange them with the
yolk upwards in a serving bowl. Spoon the sauce over
them and sprinkle with the crispy shallots and chillies.

For stars-in-the-sky, instead of deep-frying hard-
boiled eggs, use raw eggs and cook them one at a
time in a nonstick frying pan with a little oil. Splash
oil over the egg during cooking and pan-fry for
3–4 minutes or until the white has lightly browned and
the yolk is slightly firm. Arrange an egg on each plate
and add the sauce, shallots and chillies as above.

crispy rice noodles

Serves **6–8**
Preparation time **15 minutes**
Cooking time **30 minutes**

150 g (5 oz) raw **prawns**
75 g (3 oz) **rice vermicelli
    noodles**
sunflower oil, for deep-frying
200 g (7 oz) **firm bean curd
    (tofu)**, cut into matchsticks
75 g (3 oz) **shallots**, finely
    sliced
2 tablespoons **fish sauce**
2 tablespoons **pickled garlic
    juice** or **water**
1 tablespoon **lemon juice**
2 tablespoons **tomato
    ketchup**
125 g (4 oz) **caster sugar**
75 g (3 oz) **coconut**, **palm**
    or **brown sugar**, or
    6 tablespoons **clear honey**
¼ teaspoon **chilli powder**
3 small **whole pickled garlic**,
    finely sliced
2 uncooked **Salty Egg yolks**
125 g (4 oz) **bean sprouts**

To garnish
a few slices of **spring onions**
a few slices of **red chilli**

Prepare the prawns (see page 13). Put the rice noodles in a plastic bag and break into 5–7 cm (2–3 inch) pieces.

Heat 7 cm (3 inches) of oil in a wok over a medium heat. The oil is ready when a piece of noodle sinks, then immediately floats and puffs. Drop a handful of rice noodles into the oil. Turn them once and remove as soon as they swell and turn an ivory colour (it only takes seconds). Drain on kitchen paper. Fry the remaining noodles. In the same oil, deep-fry the bean curd for 7–10 minutes or until crisp. Remove and drain. Deep-fry the shallots until crispy and golden brown. Remove and drain. Deep-fry the prawns for 1–2 minutes until pink. Remove and drain.

Remove the oil from the wok. Add the fish sauce, garlic juice or water, lemon juice, ketchup and both types of sugar (or honey). Stir for 4–5 minutes over a low heat until slightly thick. Add the chilli powder.

Add half the rice noodles and gently toss with the sauce. Add the remaining noodles, bean curd, pickled garlic, prawns and shallots, tossing for 1–2 minutes until coated. Serve with salty egg yolks crumbled on top and the bean sprouts. Garnish with spring onions and chilli.

For homemade salty eggs, dissolve 200 g (7 oz) sea salt in 600 ml (1 pint) boiling water. Leave to cool. Carefully place clean duck eggs in a preserving jar without cracking the shells. Add the cool salt water, seal and leave for 3 weeks.

steamed wontons

Makes **16**
Preparation time **15 minutes**
Cooking time **30 minutes**

16 **wonton sheets**, 7 cm
  (3 inches) square
a little **sunflower oil**

Filling
6 raw **prawns**
125 g (4 oz) **minced pork**
40 g (1½ oz) **onion**, chopped
2 **garlic cloves**
5 **water chestnuts**
1 teaspoon **palm** or **light**
  muscovado sugar
1 tablespoon **light soy sauce**
1 **egg**

Make the filling by preparing the prawns (see page 13) and blending all the ingredients in a blender or food processor.

Put 1 heaped teaspoonful of the filling into the centre of a wrapper, placed over your thumb and index finger. As you push the filled wrapper down through the circle your fingers form, tighten the top, shaping it but leaving the top open. Repeat this process with all the wrappers.

Put the filled wontons on to a plate and place the plate in a steamer. Drizzle a little oil on top of the wontons, put the lid on and steam for 30 minutes.

Serve the wontons hot or warm, with a dipping sauce such as sweet chilli sauce.

For homemade sweet chilli sauce, to serve as an accompaniment, take 3 red chillies, each about 12 cm (5 inches) long, remove the stems, deseed and roughly chop them. Using a pestle and mortar or a small blender, pound or blend the chillies into a rough paste. In a small saucepan, boil 50 ml (2 fl oz) white vinegar (about 3 tablespoons), 50 g (2 oz) sugar (about 3 tablespoons) and ½ teaspoon sea salt over a medium heat for 6–7 minutes or until the mixture forms a thick syrup. Spoon the chilli paste into the syrup. Cook for 2–3 minutes, then pour into a serving bowl and sprinkle over with a few coriander leaves.

chicken wrapped in pandan leaf

Makes **25**

Preparation time **40 minutes**,
  plus marinating

Cooking time **30 minutes**

4–5 **garlic cloves**, roughly
  chopped

5 **coriander roots** and **stalks**,
  roughly chopped

750 g (1½ lb) skinless **chicken
  fillets**, cut into 20 pieces

¼ teaspoon **ground white
  pepper**

¼ teaspoon **sea salt**

2 tablespoons **oyster sauce**

1½ tablespoons **sesame oil**

1 tablespoon **plain flour**

30 **pandan leaves**, cleaned,
  dried

sunflower oil, for deep-frying

Use a pestle and mortar or a small blender to pound
or blend the garlic and coriander roots and stalks into
a paste.

Mix the chicken with the garlic paste, ground white
pepper, salt, oyster sauce, sesame oil and flour. Cover
and marinate in the refrigerator for at least 3 hours
or overnight.

Fold one of the pandan leaves, bringing the base up
in front of the tip, making a cup. Put a piece of chicken
in the fold and, moving the bottom of the leaf, wrap it
around to create a tie and enclose the chicken. Repeat
until you have used all the chicken.

Heat 7 cm (3 inches) of the oil in a wok over a medium
heat. The oil is ready when a small piece of leaf sizzles
immediately when dropped in. Deep-fry batches of
8–10 parcels for 10–12 minutes or until the parcels
feel firm and the chicken is cooked right through. Drain
on kitchen paper. Serve hot or warm with Cucumber
Relish (see page 40).

For griddled chicken sticks, omit the pandan leaves.
Add 2 red peppers, deseeded and cut into 20 pieces.
Thread the marinated chicken and peppers alternately
on to 6–8 bamboo sticks (pre-soaked in water for
30 minutes), each 18–20 cm (7–8 inches) long.
Cook the chicken sticks on the barbecue or griddle
pan, turning frequently, for 8–10 minutes or until the
meat is cooked through.

corn fritters

Makes **8**

Preparation time **12 minutes**

Cooking time **5–6 minutes each batch**

475 g (15 oz) can **sweetcorn kernels**

3 **garlic cloves**, halved

1 **coriander root**, sliced

1 small **red** or **green chilli**, roughly chopped

1 **spring onion**, finely chopped

75 g (3 oz) **rice flour** or **plain flour**

1 teaspoon **salt**

1 teaspoon **ground black pepper**

about 750 ml (1 ¼ pints) **sunflower oil**, for deep-frying

Drain the sweetcorn and make the sweetcorn liquid up to 50 ml (2 fl oz) with water. Put the sweetcorn kernels in a mixing bowl and set the measured liquid aside.

Blend the garlic, coriander root and chilli briefly in a blender or food processor.

Add the blended mixture to the sweetcorn kernels with the spring onion, flour, measured liquid, salt and pepper. Mix thoroughly to a thick consistency.

Heat the oil for deep-frying in a wok and drop in the mixture, 1 tablespoonful at a time. Cook in batches for 5–6 minutes until golden, remove from the oil and drain on kitchen paper. Repeat until all the fritters are done, then arrange them on a plate.

Serve hot, with Sweet Chilli Sauce (see page 36).

For cucumber relish, to serve as an accompaniment, mix 3 tablespoons rice wine vinegar with 1 tablespoon clear honey or sugar and ¼ teaspoon sea salt. (If using sugar, mix until it has dissolved, and set aside; you can do this an hour ahead and the sugar will be dissolved and ready to use.) Quarter and finely slice a 7 cm (3 inch) length of cucumber. Peel and finely slice 1 small carrot and 1 shallot. Remove the stem from ½ long red chilli, then deseed and finely slice it. Combine all the vegetables with the rice wine vinegar mixture in a bowl. Let it mingle and soak through for 30 minutes before serving.

pomelo salad

Serves **2**
Preparation time **8 minutes**

½ **pomelo** or 1 **grapefruit**
4 **shallots**, sliced
½ teaspoon crushed **dried chillies**
1 teaspoon **sugar**
1 tablespoon **fish sauce** or **light soy sauce**
1½–2 tablespoons **lime** or **lemon juice**

Slice a circular patch off the top of the pomelo or grapefruit, about 2 cm (¾ inch) deep (roughly the thickness of the skin). Next, score six deep lines from top to bottom, dividing the skin into six segments. Peel away each piece of skin. Remove any remaining pith and separate the segments of the fruit. Halve each segment.

Place all of the ingredients in a bowl and mix thoroughly, before serving.

For pomelo & chicken salad, mix all of the ingredients together with 200 g (7 oz) of cooked chicken, shredded into long strips, and 1 tablespoon toasted desiccated coconut. Sprinkle a handful of fresh coriander leaves over the salad before serving.

transparent noodles with prawns

Serves **4**

Preparation time **20–25 minutes**

Cooking time **10 minutes**

200 g (7 oz) medium-large raw **prawns**

125 g (4 oz) **mung bean vermicelli**

handful of **dried white** or **black fungus**

1½ tablespoons **sunflower oil**

2–3 **garlic cloves**, finely chopped

3 tablespoons **lime juice**

1 tablespoon **light soy sauce**

2 x 12 cm (5 inch) stalks **lemon grass**, finely sliced

3–4 **shallots**, finely sliced

1–2 small **bird's-eye red chillies**, finely chopped

3 **spring onions**, finely sliced

2 handfuls of **mixed salad leaves**

To garnish

coriander leaves

a few slices of **red chilli**

Prepare the prawns (see page 13). Soak the vermicelli in boiling water for 4–5 minutes or until soft. Drain and cut them to shorten their length.

Soak the fungus in boiling water for 4–5 minutes, or until soft, then drain. Discard any hard stalks and roughly chop.

Heat the oil in a wok and stir-fry the garlic over a medium heat for 1–2 minutes or until lightly browned. Spoon into a small bowl.

Cook the prawns with the lime juice and soy sauce over a medium heat for 2–3 minutes or until the prawns open and turn pink. Add the vermicelli and fungus and cook for another 2–3 minutes. Remove from the heat, add the lemon grass, shallots, chillies, spring onions and garlic oil, and mix together. Taste and adjust the seasoning.

Pile mixed salad leaves on to each serving plate. Spoon the vermicelli with prawns next to the leaves. Garnish with coriander leaves and chilli slices.

For vegetarian transparent noodles, replace the prawns with 200 g (7 oz) oyster mushrooms, cut in half if large. Alternatively, you could use 75 g (3 oz) dried small protein, minced. Soak the protein in hot water for 6–7 minutes, drain and squeeze out the water. Cook the mushrooms or protein with the lime juice and soy sauce as above before adding the remaining ingredients.

northern thai salad

Serves **4**

Preparation time **10 minutes**,
  plus soaking

Cooking time **8–10 minutes**

250 g (8 oz) **mung bean
  vermicelli**

2 tablespoons **sunflower oil**

4 **garlic cloves**, crushed

175 g (6 oz) **minced pork**

2 teaspoons **caster sugar**

125 g (4 oz) **cooked, peeled
  prawns**

2 **shallots**, finely sliced

2 tablespoons **fish sauce**

1 tablespoon **lime juice**

2 small **red chillies**, finely
  chopped

2 small **green chillies**, finely
  chopped

3 tablespoons **roasted
  peanuts**, chopped, plus
  extra to serve

2 tablespoons chopped
  coriander leaves

To garnish

2 **spring onions**, diagonally
  sliced

1 large **red chilli**, diagonally
  sliced

coriander leaves

Soak the vermicelli in warm water for about
6–7 minutes. Drain well and, using a pair of scissors,
snip them into shorter lengths.

Heat the oil in a frying pan and lightly brown the
garlic. Add the pork, crumbling and breaking up the
meat until it has separated and is cooked through.
Add 1 teaspoon of the sugar and mix together.

Remove from the heat and stir in the noodles, prawns,
shallots, fish sauce, lime juice, the remainder of the
sugar, chillies, peanuts and coriander.

Toss the ingredients together and serve in heaped
portions, garnished with spring onions, red chilli,
coriander leaves and the extra chopped roasted
peanuts.

For northern Thai salad with mushrooms,

replace the minced pork with 200 g (7 oz) mixed
oyster and shiitake mushrooms, cut in half if large
and the hard stalks removed, and 25 g (1 oz) dried
black fungus. Soak the fungus in boiling water for
4–5 minutes or until soft and then drain. Remove and
discard any hard stalks. Add the mushrooms to the
pan after the garlic has lightly browned. Stir-fry for
3–4 minutes or until cooked and slightly dry. Continue
the recipe as above.

fish salad with lemon grass

Serves **4**

Preparation time **20 minutes**

Cooking time **20 minutes**

1 tablespoon **sunflower oil**

625 g (1¼ lb) **mackerel** or **whiting**, gutted, scored with a sharp knife 3–4 times

¼ teaspoon **sea salt**

¼ teaspoon **ground black pepper**

3 x 15 cm (6 inch) stalks **lemon grass**, finely sliced

4–5 **shallots**, finely sliced

3 **spring onions**, finely sliced

2.5 cm (1 inch) piece of **fresh root ginger**, peeled, finely shredded

3–4 **kaffir lime leaves**, finely shredded

½ handful of **mint leaves**

2½ tablespoons **light soy sauce**

4 tablespoons **lime juice**

1–1½ long **red chillies**, stemmed, deseeded, finely chopped

mixed salad leaves, to serve

Line a baking sheet with foil, then drizzle and rub all over the surface with a little oil. Rub the fish with oil, salt and pepper and place on the baking sheet.

Bake in a preheated oven, 180°C (350°F), Gas Mark 4, uncovered, for 15–20 minutes or until the fish is cooked. Remove the heads (if left on) and all the bones. Break the fish, including the skin, into bite-sized chunks and put these in a mixing bowl.

Mix with the lemon grass, shallots, spring onions, ginger, kaffir lime leaves, mint leaves, soy sauce, lime juice and chillies. Taste and adjust the seasoning. Divide among 4 serving plates next to a pile of mixed salad leaves.

For tuna salad with lemon grass, replace the whole fish with 500 g (1 lb) very fresh tuna steak (sushi grade) and omit the sunflower oil, salt, kaffir lime leaves and mint leaves. Chill the tuna in the refrigerator for 2–3 hours, then finely dice it. Mix with the pepper, lemon grass, shallots, spring onions, ginger, soy sauce and 2 tablespoons lime juice. No cooking is required.

duck slices with cashew nuts

Serves **4**

Preparation time **15 minutes**, plus resting

Cooking time **20 minutes**

½ tablespoon **sunflower oil**

1 teaspoon **sesame oil**

½ teaspoon **5-spice powder**

⅛ teaspoon **sea salt**

⅛ teaspoon **ground black pepper**

2 **duck breasts**, scored with a sharp knife 3–4 times, dried

150 g (5 oz) small green **mangoes** or 1 green **apple**

10 cm (4 inch) length **cucumber**, cut in half, finely sliced

2 **tomatoes**, cut into pieces

2 **shallots**, finely sliced

2.5 cm (1 inch) piece of **fresh root ginger**, peeled, finely shredded

2½ tablespoons **light soy sauce**

2½ tablespoons **lime juice**

2 small **bird's-eye red chillies**, finely chopped

50 g (2 oz) **roasted cashew nuts**

mixed salad leaves, to serve

Rub both oils, 5-spice powder, salt and pepper over the duck breasts. Put the breasts skin side down in a cold wok, then bring it slowly up to a medium-low temperature so the white fat turns into wonderful thin, crispy, golden crackling. Cook for 10–12 minutes, then turn the breasts over and cook for a further 5 minutes. Rest for 5 minutes before slicing.

Peel and finely shred the mangoes or apple just before mixing (to prevent their colour darkening) and mix with the duck slices, cucumber, tomatoes, shallots, ginger, soy sauce, lime juice, chillies and cashew nuts. Taste and adjust the seasoning.

Pile mixed salad leaves on to each serving plate. Spoon the duck and cashew nuts on top and serve as a salad, side dish or starter.

For crispy bean curd with cashew nuts, replace the duck with 300 g (10 oz) firm bean curd (tofu). Cut the bean curd into 2.5 cm (1 inch) pieces, drain and sprinkle with the 5-spice powder, salt and pepper. Pan-fry a few at a time until crispy on all sides. Extra oil may be required for each batch. Continue as above.

sliced steak with hot & sour sauce

Serves **4**

Preparation time **5 minutes**,
   plus resting

Cooking time **8–10 minutes**

375 g (12 oz) lean **steak**
   (sirloin, rump or fillet)

½ teaspoon **sea salt**

½ teaspoon **ground black
   pepper**

1½ tablespoons **fish sauce**

4 tablespoons **lime juice**

3–4 **shallots**, finely sliced

3 **spring onions**, finely sliced

½ handful of **coriander leaves**,
   roughly chopped

¼–½ teaspoon **chilli powder**,
   depending on taste

mixed salad leaves, to serve

To garnish

mint or **coriander leaves**

a few slices of **red chilli**

Sprinkle both sides of the beef with salt and pepper. Grill or barbecue each side for 3–4 minutes (depending on the thickness of the steak), turning occasionally. Fat should drip off the meat and the meat should cook slowly enough to remain juicy and not burn. You can pan-fry the meat if you prefer. Rest it for 4–5 minutes before thinly slicing.

Mix the beef slices with the fish sauce, lime juice, shallots, spring onions, coriander and chilli powder. Taste and adjust the seasoning.

Spoon over a pile of mixed salad leaves and garnish with a few mint or coriander leaves and chilli slices.

For spicy sliced meat with cashew nut salad, you can use either beef or lamb. After you have cooked and sliced the meat as above, mix it with the other ingredients plus 2 lemon grass stalks, finely sliced, and 50 g (2 oz) roasted cashew nuts, roughly chopped. Pile over the mixed salad leaves and place a lime or lemon wedge on each serving plate.

squid salad

Serves **4**
Preparation time **15 minutes**
Cooking time **10 minutes**

500 g (1 lb) **squid tubes**
1 tablespoon **white sesame seeds**
6 **cherry tomatoes**, cut in half
2 **shallots**, finely sliced
2.5 cm (1 inch) piece of **fresh root ginger**, peeled, finely shredded
2–3 **spring onions**, finely sliced
2–3 small **bird's-eye red chillies**, finely chopped
3 **garlic cloves**, finely chopped
4 tablespoons **lime juice**
2 tablespoons **fish sauce**

To serve
½ handful of **coriander leaves**
2 handfuls of **mixed salad leaves**

Prepare the squid (see page 13).

Dry-fry the sesame seeds in a nonstick frying pan over a medium heat. Shake the pan to move the seeds around for 3–4 minutes or until they are lightly browned. Spoon into a small bowl.

Heat some water in a saucepan and bring to the boil. Add the squid, cook for 2–3 minutes, then drain (if you cook a big squid for too long it will be tough). You can save the liquid and use it later as stock.

Toss the squid, tomatoes, shallots, ginger, spring onions, chillies and garlic in the lime juice and fish sauce. Taste and adjust the seasoning.

Mix the coriander and salad leaves and pile them on to each serving plate. Spoon the squid mixture over the mixed leaves and sprinkle with the sesame seeds.

For mixed mushroom salad, replace the squid with 300 g (10 oz) mixed mushrooms. Tear the larger mushrooms in half and cook in boiling water for 2–3 minutes. Drain as much liquid as possible out of the cooked mushrooms and mix them with the ingredients, as above, adding 2 tablespoons of light soy sauce.

long aubergine salad with prawns

Serves **4**

Preparation time **20 minutes**, plus soaking

Cooking time **40 minutes**

500 g (1 lb) long green or purple **aubergines**

1 **red pepper**

125 g (4 oz) medium-large raw **prawns**

50 g (2 oz) small green **mangoes** or 1 green **apple**

3–4 **shallots**, finely sliced

40 g (1½ oz) **ground dried shrimp**

4½ tablespoons **lime juice**

1½ tablespoons **fish sauce**

1 long **red chilli**, stemmed, deseeded, finely sliced

125 ml (4 fl oz) **coconut milk**

¼ teaspoon **plain flour**

Prick the aubergines with a fork. Grill or barbecue the aubergines and pepper on a low-medium heat for 30–35 minutes. Turn until they are dark in colour (the pepper will cook faster). Set aside to cool.

Prepare the prawns (see page 13). Boil some water in a small saucepan. Cook the prawns for 2–3 minutes or until they open and turn pink, then drain (save the liquid for stock).

Peel away the dark skin of the aubergine and cut into 2.5 cm (1 inch) pieces. Peel and deseed the pepper and cut it into thin strips. Put both vegetables in a bowl with the prawns.

Peel and finely shred the mangoes or apple just before mixing (to prevent their colour darkening) and mix with the aubergine, pepper, prawns, shallots, half the dried shrimp, lime juice, fish sauce and chilli. Taste and adjust the seasoning. Leave to soak for 10 minutes.

Mix the coconut milk and flour in a small saucepan until smooth. Stir and cook over a medium heat for 2–3 minutes until thick. Spoon the aubergine mixture on to a serving plate. Drizzle the coconut milk on top. Sprinkle with the remaining dried shrimp.

For mixed sweet pepper salad with prawns, replace the aubergines with 625 g (1¼ lb) peppers of mixed colours, such as red, yellow and orange. Chargrill the peppers (this brings out the aroma in their skin) and cook the prawns as described, then mix with the other ingredients and continue as above.

green mango salad with prawns

Serves **4**

Preparation time **10 minutes**

Cooking time **4 minutes**

175 g (6 oz) medium-sized
   raw **prawns**

250 g (8 oz) green **mangoes**
   (about 3 small mangoes) or
   2 green **apples**

3–4 **shallots**, finely sliced

1–2 small **bird's-eye red
   chillies**, finely chopped

½ tablespoon **fish sauce**

25 g (1 oz) **ground dried
   shrimp**

25 g (1 oz) **roasted peanuts**

a few slices of **red chilli**, to
   garnish

Prepare the prawns (see page 13).

Bring some water to the boil in a small saucepan.
Cook the prawns in the water for 3–4 minutes or until
they open and turn pink. Drain (you can save the liquid
and use it as stock).

Peel and finely shred the mangoes or apples just
before mixing (to prevent their colour darkening) and
mix with the prawns, shallots, chillies, fish sauce, dried
shrimp and peanuts. Taste and adjust the seasoning.

Spoon on to a plate, garnish with chilli slices and
serve as a light salad on hot summer days.

For green mango salad with mixed seafood,

replace the prawns with 175 g (6 oz) mixed seafood.
Prepare the seafood if fresh (see page 13) or defrost
frozen seafood slowly in the refrigerator to preserve its
texture and flavour. Cook the seafood and mix with the
other ingredients as above. For a vegetarian version
you can use 175 g (6 oz) halved button mushrooms or
cubed aubergine.

hot & sour mushroom salad

Serves **4**
Preparation time **15 minutes**
Cooking time **10 minutes**

2½ tablespoons **lime juice**
1 tablespoon **light soy sauce**
1 teaspoon **caster sugar**
1 tablespoon **white** and **black
sesame seeds**
300 g (10 oz) mixed
mushrooms (such as oyster,
shiitake and button), hard
stalks removed, quartered if
large, left whole if small
2 **shallots**, finely sliced
1–2 small **bird's-eye red
chillies**, finely chopped
mixed salad leaves, to serve

Mix the lime juice, soy sauce and sugar and stir until
the sugar has dissolved.

Dry-fry the sesame seeds in a nonstick frying pan over
a medium heat. Shake the pan to move them around
for 3–4 minutes or until the white seeds are lightly
browned and popping. Spoon into a small bowl.

Bring some water to the boil in a saucepan. Reduce
the heat to medium, add the mushrooms and cook for
4–5 minutes. Drain well, place in a bowl with the
shallots, chillies and the sauce mixture and lightly mix
together. Taste and adjust the seasoning.

Spoon over a pile of mixed salad leaves and sprinkle
with the sesame seeds.

For hot & sour salad with wing beans, replace the
mixed mushrooms with 250 g (8 oz) wing beans (or
runner beans) and 4 cherry tomatoes. Slice the beans
into thin diagonal pieces, blanch in boiling water,
drain, then add to cold water for a minute and drain
again. Cut the tomatoes in half. Mix the beans and
tomatoes in as above. Serve with 2 tablespoons lightly
salted coconut milk poured over and sprinkle with the
sesame seeds and 50 g (2 oz) roughly chopped
salted peanuts.

bitter melon soup with prawns

Serves **4**

Preparation time **30 minutes**

Cooking time **20–25 minutes**

4 fresh or dried **shiitake mushrooms**, roughly sliced

2–3 **garlic cloves**, roughly chopped

3–4 **coriander roots** and **stalks**, roughly chopped

250 g (8 oz) **minced raw prawns**

1 tablespoon **cornflour**

¼ teaspoon **sea salt**

¼ teaspoon **ground white pepper**

400 g (13 oz) **bitter melon**, cut into 2.5 cm (1 inch) rings, deseeded

8 medium-large raw **prawns**

1.2 litres (2 pints) **vegetable stock**

20 **sun-dried goji berries** (optional)

2½ tablespoons **light soy sauce**

1 tablespoon **preserved radish**

To garnish

few slices of **spring onions**

coriander leaves

Soak the dried mushrooms in boiling water for 8–10 minutes or until soft. Cut off and discard the stalks, then drain. Use a pestle and mortar to grind and pound the garlic and coriander roots and stalks into a paste. Mix the minced prawns with the garlic paste, cornflour, salt and pepper.

Spoon the prawn mixture into the melon rings (don't overstuff the rings or they might explode during cooking). Use a cocktail stick to poke through one side of the bitter melon and out the other side. This will secure the filling inside the ring. Repeat, using the rest of the bitter melon and filling.

Prepare the whole prawns (see page 13).

Put the stock, goji berries (if using), soy sauce and preserved radish in a pan and bring to the boil. Reduce the heat to low and add the stuffed melon and mushrooms. Cook for 10–12 minutes or until the melon is tender. Add the prawns 3–4 minutes before the end of the cooking time. Taste and adjust the seasoning. Leave the sticks on the melon pieces or pull them out. Spoon into serving bowls and garnish with spring onions and coriander.

For cucumber soup with chicken, replace the bitter melon with 400 g (13 oz) cucumber, deseeded and cut into rings. Stuff the cucumber with 375 g (12 oz) minced chicken (spoon any remaining meat into the soup when you add the whole prawns). Continue as above. You could also use minced turkey or pork instead of the chicken.

glass noodle soup

Serves **2**

Preparation time **30 minutes**, plus soaking

Cooking time **6 minutes**

3–4 dried **shiitake mushrooms**

50 g (2 oz) dried sheets **bean curd (tofu)**

25 g (1 oz) dried **lily flowers**, soaked, drained, or canned **bamboo shoots**, drained and thinly sliced

125 g (4 oz) **mung bean vermicelli**, soaked, drained

600 ml (1 pint) **vegetable stock**

1½–2 tablespoons **light soy sauce**

chopped **celery leaves**, to garnish

Soak the shiitake mushrooms in 300 ml (½ pint) boiling water for 10 minutes or until soft. Drain the mushrooms then squeeze any excess water out of them, strain the liquid through a fine sieve into a bowl to remove any grit and reserve the liquid. Remove and discard the hard stalks and thinly slice the mushrooms.

Soak the dried bean curd sheets in boiling water for 6–8 minutes or until tender, drain and roughly tear the bean curd into pieces. Soak the dried lily flowers in boiling water for 8–10 minutes, then drain. Finally, soak the vermicelli in boiling water for 1–2 minutes or until soft, then drain.

Heat the stock and reserved soaking liquid to boiling point in a saucepan. Add the soy sauce, bean curd, lily flowers and mushrooms and cook for 2–3 minutes. Add the noodles and cook for another 2–3 minutes, stirring frequently. Taste and adjust the seasoning.

Spoon into a serving bowl and garnish with chopped celery leaves.

For glass noodle soup with minced protein, omit the bean curd and lily flowers. Soak 50 g (2 oz) very small minced protein in boiling water until soft, then squeeze out most of the liquid. Mix together with 1 egg yolk, 1 tablespoon chopped coriander, 1 finely chopped garlic clove, 1½ tablespoons plain flour, ¼ teaspoon each of salt and pepper, then make into balls. Heat 900 ml (1½ pints) vegetable stock and soaking liquid, 3 tablespoons light soy sauce and 1 tablespoon preserved radish. Add the protein, mushrooms and noodles. Cook for 4–5 minutes.

coconut, galangal & chicken soup

Serves **4**
Preparation time **10 minutes**
Cooking time **15 minutes**

400 ml (14 fl oz) can **coconut milk**

2 x 12 cm (5 inch) stalks **lemon grass**, bruised, sliced diagonally

5 cm (2 inches) **galangal**, thinly scraped, finely sliced

2 **shallots**, cut in half

10 **black peppercorns**, crushed

425 g (14 oz) skinless **chicken fillets**, finely sliced

2 tablespoons **fish sauce**

25 g (1 oz) **coconut, palm** or **brown sugar**, or 2 tablespoons **clear honey**

150 g (5 oz) **mixed mushrooms** (such as oyster, shiitake and button)

3 tablespoons **lime juice**

2–3 **kaffir lime leaves**, torn in half

2–3 small **bird's-eye red chillies**, lightly bruised

4 **cherry tomatoes**, with calix left on if possible

coriander leaves, to garnish

Put the coconut milk, lemon grass, galangal, shallots and peppercorns in a saucepan over a medium heat and bring to the boil.

Add the chicken, fish sauce and sugar or honey and simmer, stirring constantly, for 4–5 minutes or until the chicken is cooked.

Cut the mushrooms in half if large and discard any hard stems, then add to the saucepan and simmer for another 2–3 minutes. Add the lime juice, kaffir lime leaves and chillies. Taste and adjust the seasoning (this dish is not meant to be overwhelmingly hot, but to have a sweet, salty and sour taste). Add the cherry tomatoes in the last few seconds, taking care not to let them lose their shape.

Spoon into a serving bowl and garnish with a few coriander leaves.

For coconut & galangal soup with sweet potato, replace the chicken with 425 g (14 oz) of sweet potato. Boil the sweet potato for 8–10 minutes or until tender. Add 2½ tablespoons light soy sauce after the coconut milk mixture reaches boiling point. Add the mushrooms and cook for 2–3 minutes. Add the cooked sweet potato and warm through for 2–3 minutes and finish as above.

vermicelli soup & minced chicken

Serves **4**
Preparation time **10 minutes**
Cooking time **15 minutes**

50 g (2 oz) **mung bean vermicelli**
½ handful of **dried black fungus**
2 tablespoons **sunflower oil**
3–4 **garlic cloves**, finely chopped
500 g (1 lb) **minced chicken**
20 **coriander leaves**, finely chopped
¼ teaspoon **sea salt**
¼ teaspoon **ground white pepper**
1.2 litres (2 pints) **vegetable or chicken stock**
2 tablespoons **light soy sauce**
1 tablespoon **preserved radish**

To garnish
1–2 **spring onions**, cut into 2.5 cm (1 inch) lengths
coriander leaves

Soak the vermicelli in boiling water for 4–5 minutes or until soft. Drain, then shorten the noodles by cutting them. Soak the dried black fungus in boiling water for 4–5 minutes or until soft, then drain. Discard the hard stalks and finely chop.

Heat the oil in a small wok and stir-fry the garlic over a medium heat for 1–2 minutes or until lightly browned. Spoon into a small bowl.

Mix the chicken with the coriander, salt and pepper.

Put the stock, soy sauce and preserved radish in a saucepan and bring to the boil. Lower to medium heat and use a spoon or your wet fingers to shape the chicken mixture into small balls, about 1 cm (½ inch) across. Place them in the stock until you have used up all the mixture, then cook for 3–4 minutes. Add the noodles and black fungus and cook for another 2–3 minutes, stirring frequently. Taste and adjust the seasoning.

Spoon into a serving bowl, garnish with spring onions and coriander, and drizzle with the garlic oil.

For vermicelli soup & minced fish, replace the minced chicken with 500 g (1 lb) minced fish. Mix the fish with 1½ tablespoons plain flour so you can mould the fish into balls. Prepare and cook as above, then serve immediately.

floating purses in coconut milk

Serves **4**

Preparation time **30 minutes**

Cooking time **25–30 minutes**

375 g (12 oz) **minced chicken**

3–4 **garlic cloves**, finely chopped

6 **coriander roots** and **stalks**, 3 finely chopped

¼ teaspoon **ground white pepper**

40 **wonton sheets**, 7 cm (3 inches) square

400 ml (14 fl oz) can **coconut milk**

350 ml (12 fl oz) **vegetable** or **chicken stock**

3 x 12 cm (5 inch) stalks **lemon grass**, bruised, sliced diagonally

2.5 cm (1 inch) **galangal**, thinly scraped, finely sliced

4 **shallots**, cut in half

150 g (5 oz) **button mushrooms**, wiped

2–3 small **chillies**, bruised

2–2½ tablespoons **fish sauce**

4–5 tablespoons **lime juice**

8 **cherry tomatoes**

spinach leaves, to serve

Mix the chicken, garlic, chopped coriander and pepper together. Spoon 1 teaspoon of the mixture into the middle of each wonton sheet. Brush the edge with water and gather up, squeezing the corners together to make a little purse. Lay on a tray and repeat until you have used up all the filling and sheets.

Cook the wonton purses in boiling water for about 2–3 minutes or until they float up. Lift the purses out with a slotted spoon and drop into a bowl of cold water.

Put the coconut milk, stock, lemon grass, galangal, coriander and shallots in a saucepan and bring to the boil. Add the mushrooms and chillies and cook for 3–4 minutes. Add the fish sauce and lime juice. Taste and adjust the seasoning.

Drain the cooked wontons and spoon into the stock saucepan. Add the cherry tomatoes in the last few seconds, taking care not to let them lose their shape.

Place a handful of spinach leaves into each serving bowl. Divide and spoon the hot and sour soup with wontons into each serving bowl.

For floating purses & noodles in coconut milk, cook the purses, drain and place in a bowl of water. Cook 125 g (4 oz) mung bean vermicelli in the same boiling water for 1 minute or until soft, then drain and place in a bowl of water. Boil together the coconut milk, stock, lemon grass, galangal and coriander as above. Add the purses and noodles and adjust to taste with fish sauce and lime. Spoon into serving bowls with spinach leaves.

sour soup with mixed vegetables

Serves **4**
Preparation time **20 minutes**
Cooking time **15 minutes**

350 g (12 oz) **mixed
vegetables** (asparagus,
courgette, mushrooms, baby
sweetcord, green beans and
mangetout)
900 ml (1½ pints) **vegetable
stock**
2–3 tablespoons **Thai sour
curry paste**
20 **sun-dried goji berries**
(optional)
175 g (6 oz) **morning glory
(water spinach)**, cut into
5 cm (2 inch) pieces,
cleaned and separated top
leaves
2–2½ tablespoons **light soy
sauce**
½–1 teaspoon **palm, coconut,
brown sugar** or **honey**
4–5 tablespoons **Tamarind
Purée** (see page 90) or
3–3½ tablespoons **lime** or
lemon juice

Cut the asparagus spears into 5 cm (2 inch) pieces.
Slice the courgette and mushrooms and cut the baby
sweetcorn in half lengthways. Top and tail the green
beans and mangetout and cut diagonally.

Heat the stock with the sour curry paste and goji
berries (if using) in a saucepan on a medium heat and
bring to the boil. Add the asparagus stems, courgette
and mushrooms and cook for 3–4 minutes. Add the
asparagus tops, baby sweetcorn, green beans,
mangetout and morning glory stems, light soy sauce,
sugar and tamarind purée or lime juice and cook for
another 3–4 minutes.

Add the top leaves of morning glory and cook for
another minute or so, stirring gently occasionally. Taste
and adjust the seasoning, using a little extra light soy
sauce, sugar and tamarind purée, lime or lemon juice if
necessary. Spoon into four serving bowls and serve as
a side dish.

For homemade sour curry paste, pound or blend
3–4 chopped fresh red chillies, a 2.5 cm (1 inch)
piece of scraped and thinly sliced galangal,
4 chopped garlic cloves, 3 chopped shallots and
¼ teaspoon 5-spice powder. Continue until the
mixture forms a paste.

meat dishes

pork with sweet & sour sauce

Serves **4**
Preparation time **10 minutes**
Cooking time **30 minutes**

125 g (4 oz) **self-raising flour**
1 teaspoon **baking powder**
¼ teaspoon **sea salt**
150 ml (¼ pint) **water**
150 g (5 oz) can **pineapple
    slices in light juice**
2 tablespoons **vegetable
    stock** or **water**
½ tablespoon **cornflour**
2 tablespoons **tomato ketchup**
1 tablespoon **fish sauce**
40 g (1½ oz) **caster
    or brown sugar**, or
    3 tablespoons **clear honey**
sunflower oil, for deep-frying
275 g (9 oz) **pork fillets**, finely
    sliced
2–3 **garlic cloves**, finely
    chopped
1 **carrot**, cut into matchsticks
1 **red onion**, thinly sliced
1 **red pepper**, deseeded and
    cut into bite-sized pieces
5 cm (2 inch) length
    cucumber, cut in half
    lengthways, thinly sliced
1 **tomato**, cut into quarters
coriander leaves, to garnish

Mix the flour, baking powder and salt together in a bowl. Slowly add the water and keep stirring until you have a smooth batter. Mix about 6 tablespoons of the pineapple syrup with the stock or water, cornflour, ketchup, fish sauce and sugar or honey in a small bowl until smooth.

Heat 7 cm (3 inches) of oil in a wok over a medium heat. It is ready when a little batter sizzles immediately when dropped in. Coat half the pork in the batter and lower each slice into the oil. Deep-fry for 4–5 minutes or until nicely browned. Drain on kitchen paper. Repeat with the remaining pork.

Remove most of the oil, leaving 1½ tablespoons in the wok, and stir-fry the garlic over a medium heat for 1–2 minutes or until lightly browned. Add the carrot, onion, pepper and stir-fry for 3–4 minutes. Add the cucumber, pineapple, tomato and pineapple syrup mixture, and stir together for 1–2 minutes. Taste and adjust the seasoning. Return the pork to the pan and gently mix with the sauce.

Spoon on to 4 warm serving plates and garnish with coriander leaves.

For vegetables with sweet & sour sauce, replace the pork with 275 g (9 oz) vegetables, such as baby sweetcorn, mushrooms, topped and tailed green beans, carrots cut into matchsticks, sweet peppers cut into bite-sized pieces and sliced courgettes. Use 1½ tablespoons light soy sauce instead of fish sauce. Deep-fry the vegetables in the batter and spoon the sweet and sour sauce over them.

chicken with mixed vegetables

Serves **4** (with 2 other main dishes)
Preparation time **10 minutes**
Cooking time **6–10 minutes**

325 g (11 oz) **mixed vegetables** (including baby sweetcorn, green beans, asparagus spears and carrots)
1½ tablespoons **sunflower oil**
3–4 **garlic cloves**, finely chopped
325 g (11 oz) skinless **chicken fillets**, diced
4 tablespoons **chicken stock, vegetable stock** or **water**
2.5 cm (1 inch) piece of **fresh root ginger**, peeled, finely sliced
2 tablespoons **oyster sauce**
1½–2 tablespoons **light soy sauce**
2 **spring onions**, finely sliced
coriander leaves, to garnish

Prepare the vegetables. Cut the sweetcorn and green beans in half. Cut off the tips of the asparagus and slice each stalk into 5 cm (2 inch) lengths. Cut the carrots into matchsticks.

Blanch all the vegetables in boiling water for 1–2 minutes, remove and place them in a bowl of cold water to ensure a crispy texture, then drain.

Heat the oil in a wok or large frying pan and stir-fry the garlic over a medium heat until it is lightly browned.

Add the chicken and stir-fry for 3–5 minutes or until the meat is cooked. Add the mixed vegetables, stock or water, ginger, oyster sauce and light soy sauce and stir-fry for 2–3 minutes. Add the spring onions.

Spoon on to a serving plate, garnish with coriander leaves and serve immediately.

For homemade vegetable stock, put 2.5 litres (4 pints) cold water, 1 sweetcorn on the cob (stemmed and cleaned), 2 carrots (roughly chopped), 2 celery stalks (roughly chopped), 1 onion (outer skins removed, root cut off, quartered), 200 g (6 oz) kale or sprouting broccoli, 2.5 cm (1 inch) piece of fresh root ginger (finely sliced), 3–4 whole coriander plants (cleaned, roots lightly bruised), 30 sun-dried goji berries (optional) and 10 peppercorns (crushed) in a saucepan and bring to the boil over a medium heat. Reduce to a low heat and simmer for 45–60 minutes. Stir and skim from time to time as necessary. Strain the stock into a clean bowl.

stir-fried duck with broccoli

Serves **4**
Preparation time **20 minutes**
Cooking time **20 minutes**

275 g (9 oz) **broccoli florets**
1 tablespoon **white sesame seeds**
1½–2 tablespoons **sunflower oil**
2–3 **garlic cloves**, finely chopped
1 **onion**, thinly sliced
1 **red pepper**, deseeded, cut into bite-sized pieces
500 g (1 lb) **skinless duck fillets**, finely sliced
2.5 cm (1 inch) piece of **fresh root ginger**, peeled, finely shredded
2 tablespoons **vegetable stock** or **water**
2 tablespoons **light soy sauce**
1½ tablespoons **oyster sauce**

Blanch the broccoli florets in boiling water for 1–1½ minutes. Remove and place in a bowl of cold water or running water to ensure a crispy texture.

Dry-fry the sesame seeds in a nonstick frying pan over a medium heat. Shake the pan to move the seeds around for 3–4 minutes or until the seeds are lightly browned and popping. Spoon into a small bowl.

Heat the oil in a wok or large frying pan. Stir-fry the garlic, onion and red pepper over a medium heat for 1–2 minutes or until the garlic has lightly browned. Add the broccoli, duck, ginger, stock or water, soy sauce and oyster sauce and stir-fry for 3–4 minutes or until the duck is cooked as you like it. Taste and adjust the seasoning.

Spoon on to a warm serving plate and sprinkle with the sesame seeds. Serve with boiled rice or spoon over cooked noodles.

For stir-fried duck with water chestnuts, replace the broccoli with 125 g (4 oz) water chestnuts, each sliced in half, and 1 thinly sliced carrot. After the garlic has lightly browned add the onion, red pepper, carrots and water chestnuts, then stir-fry for 4–5 minutes. Add the duck, ginger, stock, soy sauce, oyster sauce and 2–3 tablespoons Sweet Chilli Sauce (see page 36). Stir-fry together for 3–4 minutes, taste and adjust.

pork with salty eggs

Serves **2**

Preparation time **20 minutes**

Cooking time **9 minutes**

2 **Salty Eggs** (see page 34), hard-boiled, shelled and halved

1½ tablespoons **sunflower oil**

1 **garlic clove**, chopped

75 g (3 oz) **minced pork**

200 g (7 oz) **bean sprouts**

4 tablespoons **vegetable stock**

1 tablespoon **oyster sauce**

1 tablespoon **light soy sauce**

2 large **red chillies**, diagonally sliced

1 **spring onion**, diagonally sliced

coriander leaves, to garnish

Allow the hard-boiled salty eggs to cool. Heat the oil in a wok and stir-fry the garlic for 1–2 minutes or until lightly browned. Add the pork and stir-fry for 2–3 minutes or until the pork is crumbled and separated. Add the bean sprouts, vegetable stock, oyster sauce and light soy sauce and stir-fry for 3–4 minutes.

Add the chillies, spring onion and salty eggs and lightly toss together.

Spoon into bowls and garnish with coriander leaves. Serve as a side dish.

For stir-fry pork & salty eggs with noodles, cook 300 g (10 oz) rice flake (*kua chap*) noodles or 175 g (6 oz) dried small noodles in boiling water, then drain. Rice flake noodles need 2–3 minutes, small noodles 8–10 minutes. Lightly brown 2–3 finely chopped garlic cloves and stir-fry the pork. Add bean sprouts, stir-fry for 2–3 minutes, add the noodles, stock and 2 tablespoons oyster sauce, 1½ tablespoons light soy sauce and the remaining ingredients. Sprinkle over with 50 g (2 oz) roughly chopped salty cashew nuts.

red curry with beef

Serves **4**
Preparation time **15 minutes**
Cooking time **10–15 minutes**

1½ tablespoons **sunflower oil**
2–3 tablespoons **Red Curry Paste** (see page 94)
500 g (1 lb) **fillet steak**, finely sliced
200 g (7 oz) mixed **Thai aubergines**, quartered
400 ml (14 fl oz) can **coconut milk**
50 ml (2 fl oz) **beef stock, vegetable stock** or **water**
2½ tablespoons **fish sauce**
25 g (1 oz) **coconut, palm** or **brown sugar**, or 2 tablespoons **clear honey**
2 **tomatoes**, cut in half
2–3 **kaffir lime leaves**, torn in half

To garnish
coriander leaves
a few slices of **red chilli**

Heat the oil in a wok or saucepan and stir-fry the curry paste over a medium heat for 3–4 minutes or until fragrant.

Add the beef and stir for 4–5 minutes. Add the aubergines, coconut milk, stock, fish sauce and sugar or honey and cook for about 4–5 minutes or until the aubergines are tender, stirring occasionally. Taste and adjust the seasoning. Add the tomatoes and kaffir lime leaves in the last few seconds.

Spoon into 4 serving bowls and garnish with coriander leaves and chilli slices.

For red curry with mixed vegetables, replace the steak with 500 g (1 lb) mixed vegetables (such as asparagus, green beans, baby sweetcorn and courgettes). After the curry paste has become fragrant, add the coconut milk, vegetable stock, 2½ tablespoons light soy sauce (instead of fish sauce), sugar or honey and Thai aubergines and cook for 3–4 minutes. Add the mixed vegetables and cook for another 3–4 minutes. Finish with the tomatoes and kaffir lime leaves and garnish, as above.

spicy sliced steak

Serves **4** (with 3 other main dishes)

Preparation time **10 minutes**, plus resting

Cooking time **10–14 minutes**

375 g (12 oz) **rump**, **sirloin** or **fillet steak**

1 **lemon grass stalk** (white part only), 12 cm (5 inches) long, finely sliced

3 **shallots**, finely sliced

5 **kaffir lime leaves**, finely sliced

4 tablespoons **lemon juice**

1½ tablespoons **fish sauce**

1 tablespoon **ground rice**

3–4 small **red** or **green chillies**, finely chopped, or ½–1 teaspoon **chilli powder** (or to taste)

2 tablespoons **mint leaves**, roughly chopped

mixed salad leaves, to serve

Preheat a barbecue or grill to medium (if you're using a grill, line the tray with foil). Put the beef on the grill rack and cook for 5–7 minutes on each side, turning occasionally. Leave the meat to rest for at least 5 minutes, then slice it crossways into strips.

Mix the beef, lemon grass, shallots, kaffir lime leaves, lemon juice, fish sauce, ground rice, chillies or chilli powder and mint leaves together in a bowl.

Line a serving plate with a few mixed salad leaves and spoon over the sliced steak. Serve immediately.

For spicy noodles & steak, cook 375 g (12 oz) dried small noodles, about 2.5 mm (⅛ inch) wide, in boiling water for 8–10 minutes or according to the packet instructions. Drain, then toss with 1 teaspoon fish sauce and 1 cm (½ inch) finely shredded ginger. Divide among 4 serving bowls and spoon over the sliced steak. Serve with lemon wedges and mixed salad leaves.

yellow curry with chicken

Serves **4**
Preparation time **15 minutes**
Cooking time **10–13 minutes**

1½ tablespoons **sunflower oil**
2–3 tablespoons **Yellow Curry Paste**
500 g (1 lb) skinless **chicken fillets,** finely sliced
400 ml (14 fl oz) can **coconut milk**
50 ml (2 fl oz) **vegetable stock, chicken stock** or **water**
2½ tablespoons **fish sauce**
25 g (1 oz) **palm, coconut** or **brown sugar,** or 2 tablespoons **clear honey**
150 g (5 oz) **pineapple** or 1 small can **pineapple slices in light juice,** drained, each slice cut into 5 pieces
4 **cherry tomatoes,** with calix left on if possible
2–3 **kaffir lime leaves,** torn in half

To garnish
coriander leaves

Heat the oil in a wok or saucepan. Stir-fry the yellow curry paste over a medium heat for 3–4 minutes or until fragrant.

Add the chicken and stir-fry for 4–5 minutes. Add the coconut milk, stock or water, fish sauce, sugar or honey and pineapple, and simmer over a medium heat for 3–4 minutes, stirring occasionally. Taste and adjust the seasoning. Add the tomatoes and kaffir lime leaves in the last few seconds, taking care not to let the tomatoes lose their shape.

Spoon into 4 serving bowls and garnish with coriander leaves.

For homemade yellow curry paste, stem, deseed and roughly chop 3–4 dried long red chillies, soak them in hot water for 3–4 minutes then drain. (If using fresh chillies do not soak.) Pound or blend them with a 12 cm (5 inch) stalk of finely sliced lemon grass, a 2.5 cm (1 inch) piece of scraped and finely sliced galangal, 4 chopped garlic cloves, 3 chopped shallots, 3–4 chopped coriander roots and stalks, 3 sliced kaffir lime leaves, 1 teaspoon shrimp paste, 1 teaspoon ground cumin and 1 tablespoon yellow curry powder. Continue until the mixture forms a paste. You can omit the shrimp paste for a vegetarian version. Use this quantity of curry paste to cook curries that serve 4 people.

chicken with burnt chilli paste

Serves **4**

Preparation time **20 minutes**

Cooking time **20–25 minutes**

1 tablespoon **sunflower oil**

375 g (12 oz) skinless
   chicken fillets, diced

1–1½ tablespoons **fish sauce**

2 tablespoons **chicken stock**

½ teaspoon **sugar**

125 g (4 oz) **roasted cashew
   nuts**

Burnt chilli paste

sunflower oil, for deep-frying

3–4 large dried **red chillies**,
   chopped

6 **garlic cloves**, finely
   chopped

4 **shallots**, finely sliced

1½–2 tablespoons **Tamarind
   Purée**

½–1 tablespoon **fish sauce**

25 g (1 oz) **brown sugar** or
   honey

1 tablespoon **ground dried
   shrimp** (optional)

To garnish

a few slices of **red chilli**

Thai sweet basil sprigs

Make the burnt chilli paste. Heat 5 cm (2 inches) of oil in a saucepan on a medium heat. Deep-fry the chillies for a few seconds (without burning them) to release the flavour. Spoon into a food processor or blender. Deep-fry the garlic for 3–4 minutes or until lightly browned, then add to the chillies. Deep-fry the shallots for 6–8 minutes or until lightly browned and then blend with the chillies and garlic until smooth.

Spoon the paste into a saucepan with 1½ tablespoons of the oil used for frying. Add the tamarind purée, fish sauce, sugar or honey and ground shrimp, if using, and stir-fry for 1–2 minutes or until the sugar has dissolved.

Heat the oil with 2 tablespoons of the burnt chilli paste in a wok or heavy-based frying pan and fry the chicken for 4–5 minutes or until the chicken is cooked. Add the fish sauce, stock, sugar and cashew nuts and stir-fry for another 2 minutes. Taste and adjust the seasoning, adding more chilli paste if liked.

Spoon on to a serving plate and garnish with chilli slices and a few basil sprigs.

For homemade tamarind purée, soak 50 g (2 oz) dried tamarind pulp (about 2 tablespoons) in 200 ml (7 fl oz) boiling water for 4–5 minutes. Mash with a spoon or fork to help it dissolve. Then strain the thick liquid into a small bowl and reserve the fibres in another bowl (use these if you need to strain the liquid again).

steamed curried chicken

Serves **4**
Preparation time **30 minutes**
Cooking time **15–20 minutes**

2–3 tablespoons **Red Curry
  Paste** (see page 94)
300 g (10 oz) skinless
  chicken fillets, finely sliced
400 ml (14 fl oz) can **coconut
  milk** (reserve 4 tablespoons)
2 large **eggs**
2½ tablespoons **fish sauce**
1 handful of **Thai sweet basil
  leaves**, **spinach leaves** or
  shredded cabbage
½ teaspoon **plain flour**

To garnish
2 **kaffir lime leaves**, finely
  shredded
a few slices of **red chilli**

Half-fill a wok or a steamer pan with water, cover and
bring to the boil over a medium heat.

Mix the curry paste, chicken, coconut milk, eggs and
fish sauce together. Place a few basil or spinach leaves
or shredded cabbage in the bottom of each of
4 individual bowls.

Spoon in the chicken mixture until three-quarters full.
Place the bowls in a traditional bamboo steamer basket
or on a steamer rack inside the wok. Cover and steam
for 15–20 minutes.

Meanwhile, mix the flour and reserved coconut milk
in a small saucepan until smooth. Stir and cook over
a medium heat for 2–3 minutes or until thick. Spoon a
little over the steamed chicken.

Sprinkle with the kaffir lime leaves and chilli slices,
and serve.

For steamed curried fish & spirulina, replace
the red curry paste with 2–3 tablespoons green curry
paste (see page 200) and replace the chicken with
300 g (10 oz) minced white fish such as haddock,
cod or coley. Mix the curry paste, fish, coconut milk,
eggs, fish sauce, 50 g (2 oz) roughly chopped
cashew nuts and 1 tablespoon spirulina together.
Spoon into 4 individual bowls until three-quarters full.
Cover with the basil leaves and place a slice of salty
egg (see page 34) flat side down in the middle.
Steam as above, spoon over the coconut milk and
sprinkle with a few slices of chilli.

curried chicken & baby aubergines

Serves **4** (with 2 other main dishes)
Preparation time **5 minutes**
Cooking time **10–12 minutes**

1½ tablespoons **sunflower oil**
2–3 tablespoons **Red Curry Paste**
475 g (15 oz) skinless **chicken fillets**, thinly sliced
250 ml (8 fl oz) can **coconut milk**, shaken well
200 ml (7 fl oz) **chicken stock**
200 g (7 oz) **Thai aubergines**
2½–3 tablespoons **fish sauce**
25 g (1 oz) **palm** or **coconut sugar**
5 **kaffir lime leaves**, torn in half
Thai sweet basil leaves, to garnish

Heat the oil in a wok or large frying pan and stir-fry the curry paste over a medium heat for 2 minutes or until it is fragrant.

Add the chicken and stir-fry for 2–3 minutes. Add the coconut milk, stock, aubergines, fish sauce, sugar and kaffir lime leaves and cook for 5–7 minutes.

Spoon into a serving bowl, garnish with Thai sweet basil leaves and serve immediately.

For homemade red curry paste, stem, deseed and roughly chop 3–4 dried long red chillies and soak them in hot water for 3–4 minutes, then drain. Pound or blend them with a 12 cm (5 inch) stalk of finely sliced lemon grass, a 2.5 cm (1 inch) piece of scraped and finely sliced galangal, 4 chopped garlic cloves, 3 chopped shallots, 3–4 chopped coriander roots and stalks, 3 sliced kaffir lime leaves, 1 teaspoon shrimp paste and 1 teaspoon ground coriander. Continue until the mixture forms a paste. You can omit the shrimp paste for a vegetarian version. Use this quantity of curry paste to cook curries that serve 4 people.

beef with black bean sauce

Serves **4**

Preparation time **10 minutes**

Cooking time **8–11 minutes**

1½–2 tablespoons **black bean sauce**, roughly mashed

100 ml (3½ fl oz) **beef stock, vegetable stock** or **water**

1 tablespoon **fish sauce**

2 tablespoons **oyster sauce**

½ tablespoon **cornflour**

1½ tablespoons **sunflower oil**

3–4 **garlic cloves**, finely chopped

500 g (1 lb) **beef fillets**, finely sliced

1 **red** or **yellow pepper**, deseeded, cut into bite-sized pieces

1 **onion**, thinly sliced

2–3 **spring onions**, cut into 2.5 cm (1 inch) pieces

coriander leaves, to garnish

Mix the black bean sauce, stock or water, fish sauce, oyster sauce and cornflour together in a small bowl.

Heat the oil in a wok or large frying pan and stir-fry the garlic over a medium heat for 1–2 minutes or until lightly browned. Add the beef and stir-fry for 4–5 minutes.

Add the pepper and onion and stir-fry for another 3–4 minutes. Add the black bean sauce mixture and spring onion and toss together. Taste and adjust the seasoning.

Spoon on to 4 warm serving plates and garnish with coriander leaves.

For mixed vegetables with black bean sauce,

replace the beef with 500 g (1 lb) mixed vegetables such as mushrooms, courgettes, white radish, carrots (cut into matchsticks), baby sweetcorn, green beans, roughly chopped spring green leaves and bean sprouts. Use vegetable stock and replace the fish and oyster sauces with 1½ tablespoons light soy sauce. After the garlic has lightly browned, add the mushrooms, courgettes, radish and carrots and stir-fry for 3–4 minutes. Add the sweetcorn, green beans, spring green leaves and bean sprouts and stir-fry for another 3–4 minutes. Continue as above.

thai barbecued chicken

Serves **4–6**
Preparation time **30–40 minutes**, plus marinating
Cooking time **10–40 minutes**

12 cm (5 inch) **lemon grass stalk**, finely sliced
5 cm (2 inch) piece of fresh **galangal**, peeled, finely chopped
4 **garlic cloves**, crushed
4 **shallots**, finely chopped
4 **coriander roots** and **stalks**, finely chopped
1.5 kg (3 lb) **chicken**, spatchcocked, or a mixture of **chicken breasts**, **thighs** and **legs**, cleaned and dried
150 ml (¼ pint) thick **coconut milk**
1½ tablespoons **fish sauce**
1 teaspoon **ground pepper**
lime wedges, to serve
chive flowers, to garnish

Pound the lemon grass, galangal, garlic, shallots and coriander in a pestle and mortar or use a food processor to blend it to a paste. Add the coconut milk, fish sauce and pepper and mix until well blended. Pour this coconut marinade over the chicken, cover and leave to marinate for at least 3 hours or overnight in the refrigerator. Turn the chicken occasionally.

Remove the chicken from the marinade, place it on a hot barbecue and cook for 30–40 minutes for spatchcocked chicken and 10–15 minutes for chicken pieces, turning and basting regularly with the remaining marinade. The whole chicken is cooked when a skewer inserted in one of the legs reveals clear juices.

Leave the chicken to stand for 5 minutes, then chop it into small pieces.

Serve with Sweet Chilli Sauce (see page 36), white Sticky Rice (see page 220) and lime wedges. Garnish with chive flowers and eat with fingers.

For southern spicy Thai barbecued chicken, add 3 fresh or 3–4 long red chillies (about 12 cm/5 inches long) and 2 teaspoons ground turmeric. Soak the dried chillies in boiling water for 4–5 minutes or until soft, then drain. Pound or blend them and the ground turmeric with the rest of the ingredients. Marinate and grill as above and serve with sticky rice and lime wedges.

stir-fried chicken & cashew nuts

Serves **4**
Preparation time **10 minutes**
Cooking time **about 25 minutes**

5 tablespoons **vegetable** or **chicken stock** or **water**
1½ tablespoons **fish sauce**
2 tablespoons **oyster sauce**
½ teaspoon **sugar**
1 teaspoon **cornflour**
75 g (3 oz) **cashew nuts**
2 tablespoons **sunflower oil**
1–2 dried **red chillies**, about 12 cm (5 inches) long, stemmed, deseeded, chopped into 1 cm (½ inch) lengths
2–3 **garlic cloves**, finely chopped
500 g (1 lb) skinless **chicken fillets**, finely sliced
1 **carrot**, sliced into matchsticks
1 **red** or **yellow pepper**, deseeded, cut into bite-sized pieces
1 **onion**, thinly sliced
2–3 **spring onions**, cut into 2.5 cm (1 inch) long pieces
ground black pepper
coriander leaves, to garnish

Mix the stock or water, fish sauce, oyster sauce, sugar and cornflour in a small bowl until smooth.

Dry-fry the cashew nuts in a nonstick frying pan on a low heat. Shake the pan to move them around for 8–10 minutes or until lightly browned. Remove from the pan.

Heat 1½ tablespoons of oil in a wok and stir-fry the chillies over a medium heat for a few seconds. They should darken but not blacken and burn. Remove and drain on kitchen paper. Heat the remaining oil in the wok, adding extra if required, and stir-fry the garlic for 1–2 minutes or until lightly browned. Add the chicken and stir-fry for 4–5 minutes. Add the carrot, pepper and onion and stir-fry for another 3–4 minutes.

Stir the sauce mixture, pour it in and stir-fry together for another minute or so. Taste and adjust the seasoning. Add the cashew nuts, chillies and spring onions. Sprinkle with ground black pepper and toss well.

Spoon on to a warm serving plate and garnish with coriander leaves.

For stir-fried bean curd & sweet chilli sauce,
replace the chicken with 500 g (1 lb) firm bean curd, cut into 1 cm (½ inch) cubes. Pan-fry the bean curd with a little oil until lightly browned on each side. Replace the fish sauce, oyster sauce, sugar and dried red chillies with 3–3½ tablespoons light soy sauce and 2 tablespoons sweet chilli sauce (see page 36). Add the bean curd and sauce mixture to the pan after frying the carrot, pepper and onion. Warm through.

grilled beef with spicy sauce

Serves **1**
Preparation time **2 minutes**
Cooking time **6 minutes** (for
medium rare)

300 g (10 oz) **sirloin steak**

Spicy sauce
½ **tomato**, finely chopped
¼ **red onion**, finely chopped
½–1 teaspoon **dried ground
chilli**
2½ tablespoons **fish sauce**
2 tablespoons **lime juice** or
Tamarind Purée (see page
90)
1 teaspoon **palm** or **light
muscovado sugar**
1 teaspoon **ground rice**
1 tablespoon **beef or
vegetable stock**

To garnish
Thai sweet basil leaves
coriander leaves
a few slices of **red chilli**

Put the steak under a preheated hot grill and cook,
turning it once, according to your taste.

While it is cooking, mix together all the sauce
ingredients in a bowl.

Slice the steak when it is ready, slice it up and
arrange on a serving dish and garnish with the basil,
coriander and chillies. Serve the sauce separately.

For chilli grilled beef, mix thinly sliced grilled steak
with 4 finely sliced shallots, 3 finely sliced spring
onions, 2 tablespoons fish sauce, 5 tablespoons
lime or lemon juice, ½ teaspoon ground black pepper,
¼–½ teaspoon chilli powder and a small handful of
fresh coriander leaves. Serve with mixed salad leaves.

spicy chicken with tomatoes

Serves **4**

Preparation time **10 minutes**

Cooking time **about 10 minutes**

1½ tablespoons **sunflower oil**

3–4 **garlic cloves**, finely chopped

1–2 small **red** or **green chillies**, lightly bruised

500 g (1 lb) skinless **chicken fillets**, finely sliced

1 **red onion**, thinly sliced

4 tablespoons **chicken stock**, **vegetable stock** or **water**

1 tablespoon **fish sauce**

3 tablespoons **oyster sauce**

2 medium-sized **tomatoes**, quartered

1 handful of **Thai sweet basil leaves**

Heat the oil in a wok or large frying pan. Stir-fry the garlic over a medium heat for 1–2 minutes or until lightly browned. Add the chillies, chicken, onion, stock or water, fish sauce and oyster sauce. Stir-fry for 4–5 minutes or until the meat is cooked.

Add the tomatoes and basil leaves and stir-fry until the basil begins to wilt. Taste and adjust the seasoning.

Spoon on to a serving plate.

For spicy chicken with spring greens & tomatoes, after lightly browning the garlic add the chillies, 375 g (12 oz) chicken and onion, stir-fry for 3–4 minutes. Add 300g (10 oz) of roughly chopped spring green leaves (without stalks) with the rest of the ingredients and stir-fry for another 4–5 minutes or until the leaves are tender. You may need to add a little more fish sauce if required.

pork with ginger & water chestnuts

Serves **4**

Preparation time **20 minutes**

Cooking time **10–15 minutes**

1 handful of **dried black fungus**

1½–2 tablespoons **sunflower oil**

2–3 **garlic cloves**, finely chopped

500 g (1 lb) **pork fillets**, finely sliced

1 **red onion**, thinly sliced

150 g (5 oz) can **water chestnuts**, drained and sliced

2.5 cm (1 inch) piece of **fresh root ginger**, peeled, finely shredded

4 tablespoons **vegetable stock** or **water**

1 tablespoon **fish sauce**

1 tablespoon **oyster sauce**

2 **spring onions**, cut into 2.5 cm (1 inch) lengths

To garnish
ground white pepper
coriander leaves
a few slices of **red chilli**

Soak the dried fungus in boiling-hot water for 3–4 minutes or until soft, then drain. Remove and discard the hard stalks and roughly chop.

Heat the oil in a wok or large frying pan. Stir-fry the garlic over a medium heat for 1–2 minutes or until lightly browned. Add the pork and onion and stir-fry for 4–5 minutes or until the pork is cooked.

Add the water chestnuts, ginger, fungus, stock or water, fish sauce, oyster sauce and spring onions. Stir-fry for another 2–3 minutes. Taste and adjust the seasoning.

Spoon on to a warm serving plate, then sprinkle with ground white pepper, coriander and chilli slices.

For spicy pork with bamboo shoots, heat the oil with 2 tablespoons of red curry paste (see page 94) until fragrant. Add the pork and stir-fry for 4–5 minutes. Add 150 g (5 oz) sliced canned bamboo shoots, 2 tablespoons fish sauce, 2 tablespoons oyster sauce and 1 tablespoon coconut or palm sugar and adjust seasoning to taste.

red curry duck

Serves **3–4**

Preparation time **12–15 minutes**

Cooking time **9 minutes**

¼ roast **duck**

1 tablespoon **sunflower oil**

1½ tablespoons **Red Curry Paste** (see page 94)

150 ml (¼ pint) **coconut milk**

4 tablespoons **chicken stock**

1 tablespoon **palm** or **soft brown sugar**

1½–2 tablespoons **fish sauce**

3 **kaffir lime leaves**, torn, or ¼ teaspoon grated **lime rind**

65 g (2½ oz) fresh or frozen **peas**

2 **tomatoes**, finely diced

125 g (4 oz) fresh or canned **pineapple**, cut into chunks, plus extra to serve

noodles, to serve

To garnish

a few slices of **red chilli**

strips of **spring onion**

Take the skin and meat off the duck, chop it into bite-sized pieces and set aside.

Heat the oil in a wok, add the curry paste and fry, stirring, for 2 minutes or until it is fragrant. Add the coconut milk, stock, ½ tablespoon sugar and 1½ tablespoons fish sauce and simmer for 2 minutes.

Add the duck, kaffir lime leaves, peas, tomatoes and pineapple and cook for another 4–5 minutes, stirring occasionally. Taste and adjust the seasoning, using the rest of the sugar and fish sauce if necessary.

Serve with the extra pineapple and noodles, if liked, garnished with a few slices of red chilli and spring onion strips.

For red curry with prawns & asparagus, replace the roasted duck, frozen peas and pineapple with 300 g (10 oz) raw medium prawns. Prepare the prawns (see page 13) and 150 g (5 oz) asparagus spears, each spear sliced into 5 cm (2 inch) pieces. Add the asparagus after the curry paste has become fragrant and stir-fry together for 3–4 minutes. Add the coconut milk, stock, sugar, 1½ tablespoons fish sauce, the prawns and the asparagus. Simmer for another 3 minutes or until the prawns are cooked as you like them.

duck & lemon grass sauce

Serves **4–6**

Preparation time **30–40 minutes**, plus drying and resting

Cooking time **2–3 hours**

2 kg (4 lb) **duck**, with giblets

4 x 12 cm (5 inch) stalks **lemon grass**, crushed, roughly sliced

4 **spring onions**, cut in half

3–4 **garlic cloves**, cut in half

15 **shallots**, cut in half

1 teaspoon **allspice powder**

4 tablespoons **oyster sauce**

1.2 litres (2 pints) **vegetable stock**

2 **carrots**, roughly chopped

2.5 cm (1 inch) piece of **fresh root ginger**, finely sliced

10 **black peppercorns**, crushed

1½ tablespoons **plain flour**

2 tablespoons **oyster sauce**

1–1½ tablespoons **light soy sauce**

1–2 tablespoons **coconut, palm** or **brown sugar**

To garnish

slices of **cucumber**

coriander leaves

Clean the duck, prick all over with a fork and dry at room temperature for 2 hours or overnight.

Mix half of the lemon grass, half of the spring onions, garlic, 6 shallot halves and allspice powder together. Spoon the mixture into the duck and rub 1 tablespoon of oyster sauce on the outside. Roast in a preheated oven, 200°C (400°F), Gas Mark 6, uncovered, for 30 minutes. Lower the heat to 180°C (350°F), Gas Mark 4, and roast for 2 hours until the skin is crispy.

Meanwhile, clean the giblets and bring to the boil with the stock, the remaining lemon grass and spring onions, carrots, the remaining shallots, ginger and black peppercorns. Lower the heat and simmer for 1½ hours, skimming occasionally. Strain the stock into a clean bowl. Remove the giblets, discard the solids and allow to cool.

Remove the duck from the oven and tip the juice from the body cavity into a saucepan. Rest the duck for 15–20 minutes. Discard the fat and add the duck gravy to the stock saucepan.

Mix the flour with a little stock in a bowl. Simmer and stir the remaining stock, oyster sauce, light soy sauce and sugar on a low heat. Add the flour liquid and stir until it thickens. Taste and adjust the seasoning.

Remove the meat from the duck and divide it on top of boiled jasmine rice (see page 126). Spoon the sauce over the duck and garnish with cucumber and coriander.

chiang mai jungle curry with beef

Serves **4**

Preparation time **10 minutes**

Cooking time **about 25 minutes**

1½ tablespoons **sunflower oil**

2–3 tablespoons **Red Curry Paste** (see page 94)

1 teaspoon **ground turmeric**

¼ teaspoon **allspice powder**

500 g (1 lb) lean **beef**, thinly sliced

400 ml (14 fl oz) can **coconut milk**

250 ml (7 fl oz) **beef** or **vegetable stock**

2½–3 tablespoons **fish sauce**

50–65 g (2–2½ oz) **coconut, palm** or **brown sugar** or 4–5 tablespoons **clear honey**

4–5 tablespoons **Tamarind Purée** (see page 90) or 3–3½ tablespoons **lime juice**

To garnish

½ **red pepper**, cut into thin strips

2 **spring onions**, shredded

Heat the oil in a saucepan and stir-fry the curry paste, ground turmeric and allspice powder over a medium heat for 3–4 minutes or until fragrant.

Add the beef and stir-fry for 4–5 minutes. Add the coconut milk, stock, fish sauce, sugar or honey, tamarind purée or lime juice. Gently simmer over a low heat for 10–15 minutes or until the beef is soft and tender. Taste and adjust the seasoning. If you have reduced the sauce too much just add a little stock or water.

Spoon into serving bowls, garnish with strips of red pepper and spring onion and serve with rice.

For chiang mai pork curry, replace the beef with 750 g (1½ lb) pork belly cut into 2.5 cm (1 inch) pieces. Add to the saucepan after the curry paste is fragrant and cook for 4–5 minutes. Add the coconut milk, 500 ml (17 fl oz) vegetable stock, 20 whole small shallots, 50 g (2 oz) roasted peanuts, 2.5 cm (1 inch) piece of fresh root ginger, shredded, the fish sauce, sugar, tamarind purée and simmer for 45 minutes–1 hour, or until the pork is tender. Cook this a day ahead so you can discard any fat that has rise to the top and reheat it the next day. Spoon into serving bowls and garnish with a few slices of red chilli.

duck & lychee curry

Serves **4**
Preparation time **15 minutes**
Cooking time **15 minutes**

1½ tablespoons **sunflower oil**
2–3 tablespoons **Red Curry
Paste** (see page 94)
500 g (1 lb) chopped and
boned **roasted duck** (about
½ duck)
400 ml (14 fl oz) can **coconut
milk**
50 ml (2 fl oz) **vegetable
stock** or **water**
2–½ tablespoons **fish sauce**
15–25 g (½–1 oz) **coconut,
palm** or **brown sugar**, or
2 tablespoons **clear honey**
425 g (14 oz) can **lychees in
light juice**, drained
4 **cherry tomatoes**, with calix
left on if possible
2–3 **kaffir lime leaves**, torn in
half

Heat the oil in a wok or saucepan and stir-fry the
curry paste over a medium heat for 3–4 minutes or
until fragrant.

Add the roasted duck and stir for 3–4 minutes. Add
the coconut milk, stock or water, fish sauce and
sugar or honey and simmer over a medium heat for
3–4 minutes or until the sugar has dissolved. Add the
lychees, tomatoes and kaffir lime leaves in the last few
seconds, taking care not to let the tomatoes lose their
shape. Taste and adjust the seasoning.

Spoon into 4 serving bowls and serve with cooked
rice and steamed vegetables, or spoon over cooked
noodles.

For chicken balls & lychee curry, replace the
duck with 500 g (1 lb) minced chicken and a
handful of dried black fungus. Soak the fungus in
boiling water for 5 minutes, drain, discard any hard
stalks and finely chop. Mix the chicken and fungus
with 4 garlic cloves, 4 coriander roots and stalks,
20 finely chopped coriander leaves and ¼ teaspoon
sea salt. When the curry paste has become fragrant,
add the coconut milk, stock, fish sauce and sugar.
Drop spoonfuls of the chicken mixture into the
sauce until you use up all the mixture. Simmer for
2–3 minutes then continue cooking as above.

massaman curry

Serves **4**
Preparation time **20 minutes**
Cooking time **25–35 minutes**

1½–2 tablespoons **vegetable oil**
2 **shallots**, finely chopped
2 tablespoons **Massaman curry paste**
25–50 g (1–2 oz) **unsalted roasted peanuts**
500 g (1 lb) **chicken** or **beef**, diced
400 g (14 fl oz) can **coconut milk**
150 ml (¼ pint) **chicken** or **vegetable stock**
2–2½ tablespoons **fish sauce**
40–50 g (1½–2 oz) **palm, coconut** or **brown sugar**
140 g (5 oz) **potato**, diced
1 **onion**, sliced lengthways
2½–3 tablespoons **Tamarind Purée** (see page 90)
2 **kaffir lime leaves**, shredded
red chillies, chopped, to garnish

Heat the oil in a saucepan and lightly brown the shallots for 2–3 minutes. Add the curry paste and peanuts and stir-fry for another 3–4 minutes or until fragrant.

Add the chicken or beef and stir-fry for 4–5 minutes. Add the coconut milk, stock, 2 tablespoons fish sauce and 40 g (1½ oz) sugar. Simmer for 10–15 minutes or until the meat starts to get tender.

Add the potato, onion, 2½ tablespoons tamarind purée and continue cooking for another 5–6 minutes or until the potatoes are tender. Adjust to taste, using the rest of the fish sauce, sugar and tamarind purée if necessary.

Spoon into serving bowls, garnished with shredded kaffir lime leaves and chopped chilli.

For homemade Massaman curry paste, stem, deseed and roughly chop 3–4 dried long red chillies and soak them in hot water for 3–4 minutes, then drain. (If using fresh chillies do not soak.) Pound or blend them with a 12 cm (5 inch) finely sliced stalk of lemon grass, a 2.5 cm (1 inch) piece of thinly scraped, finely sliced fresh galangal, 4 chopped garlic cloves, 3 chopped shallots, 3–4 chopped coriander roots and stalks, 3 finely chopped kaffir lime leaves, 1 teaspoon shrimp paste and 2 teaspoons of 5-spice powder. Blend until the mixture forms a paste. Use this quantity of curry paste to cook curries that serve 4 people.

raw vegetables & dipping sauce

Serves **4**
Preparation time **15 minutes**
Cooking time **10 minutes**

about 500 g (1 lb) **mixed raw
    vegetables**
2–3 tablespoons **yellow bean
    sauce**
200 g (7 oz) **minced pork**
250 g (8 oz) **minced prawns**
2 **shallots**, finely chopped
150 ml (¼ pint) **coconut milk**
2–2½ tablespoons **Tamarind
    Purée** (see page 90)
½–1 tablespoon **fish sauce**
15–25 g (½–1 oz) **coconut,
    palm** or **brown sugar** or
    1–2 tablespoons **clear
    honey**
1 large **red chilli**, sliced
    lengthways, to garnish

Slice the vegetables into bite-sized pieces.

Mash the yellow bean sauce with a fork until it
becomes a rough paste. Mix the paste together with
the minced pork, prawn and shallots.

Heat the coconut milk on a low–medium heat for
3–4 minutes. Add in the yellow bean paste mixture
and stir until combined with the coconut milk. Add the
tamarind purée, fish sauce and sugar, stir for a few
more minutes and then adjust to taste. It should be
3-flavoured – sweet, sour and lightly salty (from the
yellow bean sauce).

Spoon into dipping bowls, sprinkle with the chilli and
serve warm with the crunchy vegetables.

For pork & bean curd dipping sauce, replace the
prawns with 250 g (8 oz) diced firm bean curd (tofu).
Mix the yellow bean paste together with the minced
pork, bean curd and shallots and cook as above.
Serve with raw vegetables as an extra dish with
a meal.

seafood dishes

crispy fish with green beans

Serves **4**

Preparation time **10 minutes**,
  plus drying and resting

Cooking time **40 minutes**

625 g (1¼ lb) **mackerel**,
  gutted, cleaned, dried
sunflower oil, for deep-frying
1½–2 tablespoons **Red Curry**
  Paste (see page 94)
15 g (½ oz) **soya protein**
  mince
175 g (6 oz) **green beans**, cut
  into 2.5 cm (1 inch) lengths
1 tablespoon **fish sauce**
15 g (½ oz) **coconut**, **palm**
  or **brown sugar**, or
  1 tablespoon **clear honey**
1 tablespoon **ground dried**
  shrimp

To garnish
5 **kaffir lime leaves**, finely
  shredded
a few slices of **red chilli**

Barbecue or grill the fish over a medium heat for
6–8 minutes each side until cooked. Let it cool
completely. Remove the heads and remaining bones.
Use a fork to comb and fluff out the flesh into very
small pieces and spoon on to a tray. Dry at room
temperature for 2–3 hours, or more quickly in an
oven on a low setting.

Heat 7 cm (3 inches) of oil in a wok over a medium
heat. It is ready when a small piece of fish sizzles
immediately when dropped in. Deep-fry in 3–4 batches,
cooking each for 3 minutes until crispy. Use 2 spoons
to flip the fish and cook for another 1–2 minutes. Drain
on kitchen paper.

Soak the soya protein mince in hot water for 6–7
minutes. Drain, squeezing out the water completely.

Heat 1½ tablespoons of oil in a wok. Stir-fry the curry
paste over a medium heat for 3–4 minutes until
fragrant. Add the protein mince, beans, fish sauce,
sugar or honey and dried shrimp. Stir-fry for
3–4 minutes. Taste and adjust the seasoning.

Divide the crispy fish between 4 plates and spoon the
chilli beans beside it. Garnish with kaffir lime leaves
and chilli slices.

For crispy fish with vegetables, use 175 g (6 oz) of
mixed baby sweetcorn, courgettes and mangetout
instead of the green beans. Cut the baby sweetcorn
lengthways, cut the courgettes into matchstick pieces
(about 2.5 cm/1 inch long) and cut the mangetout
diagonally. Stir-fry as above.

black sesame seeds with prawns

Serves **4** (with 2 other main
dishes)
Preparation time **10 minutes**
Cooking time **about
10 minutes**

250 g (8 oz) **raw prawns**
½ tablespoon **black sesame
seeds**
1½ tablespoons **sunflower oil**
2–3 **garlic cloves**, finely
chopped
200 g (7 oz) **water chestnuts**,
drained and thinly sliced
125 g (4 oz) **mangetout**,
trimmed
2 tablespoons **vegetable
stock**, **seafood stock** or
water
1 tablespoon **light soy sauce**
1 tablespoon **oyster sauce**

Prepare the prawns (see page 13).

Dry-fry the black sesame seeds in a small pan for
1–2 minutes or until they are fragrant, then set
them aside.

Heat the oil in a wok or large frying pan and stir-fry the
garlic over a medium heat until it is lightly browned.

Add the prawns, water chestnuts and mangetout and
stir-fry over a high heat for 1–2 minutes. Add the stock,
soy sauce and oyster sauce and stir-fry for another
2–3 minutes or until the prawns open and turn pink.
Stir in the fried sesame seeds and serve immediately.

For homemade seafood stock, put 1.8 litres
(3 pints) cold water, 1 onion (outer skins removed,
root cut off, quartered), 1 carrot (roughly chopped),
3 garlic cloves (unpeeled, lightly bruised), 20 cm
(8 inches) lemon grass stalks (bruised, roughly sliced),
2.5 cm (1 inch) piece of fresh root ginger (peeled,
finely sliced), 3 whole coriander plants (cleaned,
the roots lightly bruised), 30 sun-dried goji berries
(optional), 5 black peppercorns (crushed) and 250 g
(8 oz) fish heads, tails and bones (cleaned) or mixed
fish bones and prawn shells in a large saucepan. Heat
over a medium heat to boiling point. Reduce to a low
heat and simmer for 10 minutes. During simmering,
skim from time to time. Add the fish heads, tails and
bones, simmering for another 10–15 minutes. Strain
the stock into a clean bowl.

quail eggs with green bean nests

Serves **4**

Preparation time **15–20 minutes**

Cooking time **about 25 minutes**

175 g (6 oz) medium-sized raw **prawns**

12 **quail eggs**

sunflower oil, for deep-frying

1½–2 tablespoons **Red Curry Paste** (see page 94)

175 g (6 oz) **green beans**, cut into 2.5 cm (1 inch) diagonal lengths

1 tablespoon **fish sauce**

15 g (½ oz) **coconut, palm** or **brown sugar**, or

1 tablespoon **clear honey**

2–3 **kaffir lime leaves**, finely shredded, to garnish

Prepare the prawns (see page 13).

Lower the eggs into a saucepan of water and bring to the boil, then reduce the heat and simmer for 5 minutes. Drain, crack the shells slightly and cool in cold water. Peel off the shells.

Heat 5 cm (2 inches) of oil in a wok over a medium heat. The oil must not be too hot. It is ready when a small piece of green bean sizzles immediately when dropped in. Add the eggs carefully and deep-fry for 6–8 minutes or until golden brown. Remove and drain on kitchen paper. Deep-fry the prawns for 1–2 minutes. Remove and drain.

Remove most of the oil but leave 1½ tablespoons in the wok and stir-fry the curry paste over a medium heat for 3–4 minutes or until fragrant. Add the beans, fish sauce and sugar or honey and stir-fry for 3–4 minutes. Add the prawns, then taste and adjust the seasoning.

Spoon the beans and prawns on to 4 warm serving plates, arrange the quail eggs on top and garnish with kaffir lime leaves.

For quail eggs nests with mixed vegetables, replace the green beans with 175 g (6 oz) of courgettes, asparagus and baby sweetcorn. You will need to cut courgettes into matchsticks and thin asparagus into 2.5 cm (2 inch) lengths, but you can leave baby sweetcorn whole. Cook as above.

garlic chive flowers with prawns

Serves **4**

Preparation time **10 minutes**

Cooking time **about
5 minutes**

1–1½ tablespoons **sunflower
oil**

2–3 **garlic cloves**, finely
chopped

375 g (12 oz) **flowering garlic
Chinese chives**, cut into
7 cm (3 inch) lengths
(discard the hard ends of
the stems)

1 tablespoon **light soy sauce**

2 tablespoons **oyster sauce**

250 g (8 oz) small raw
prawns, peeled, roughly
chopped

a few slices of **red chilli**, to
garnish

Heat the oil in a wok or large frying pan, add the
garlic and stir-fry over a medium heat until lightly
browned. Add the chives, light soy sauce and oyster
sauce and stir-fry for 2–3 minutes.

Add the prawns to the wok and stir-fry for 3 minutes
or until cooked as you like. Spoon on to a serving plate
and garnish with chilli slices.

Serve immediately with boiled Jasmine rice or cooked
noodles.

For jasmine rice, to serve as an accompaniment, put
500 g (1 lb) jasmine rice in a bowl with some clean
water. Scoop it through your fingers 4–5 times and
drain. Scoop and drain once more. Place the rice in a
nonstick saucepan and add 900 ml (1½ pints) water
or vegetable stock. Bring to a high heat and stir the
rice frequently until it reaches boiling point. Turn the
heat down as low as possible, then cover, leaving a
small gap between the lid and the side of the pan.
Simmer gently for 10–15 minutes or until the liquid
has been absorbed. Remove from the heat and allow
to stand for another 10–15 minutes. Remove the
lid, stir the rice gently to fluff and separate the
grains and serve.

steamed fish with preserved plums

Serves **4**
Preparation time **30 minutes**
Cooking time **20 minutes**

1 kg (2 lb) **whole fish** (such
    as pomfret, plaice, snapper
    or sea bass), cleaned, scaled
    (if necessary), gutted, scored
    3–4 times with a sharp knife
3.5 cm (1½ inch) piece of
    fresh root ginger, peeled,
    finely shredded
50 g (2 oz) **button
    mushrooms**, wiped, thinly
    sliced
50 g (2 oz) **smoked bacon**,
    cut into thin strips
4 **spring onions**, cut into
    2.5 cm (1 inch) lengths
2 small **preserved plums**,
    lightly bruised
2 tablespoons **light soy
    sauce**
pinch of **ground white pepper**

To garnish
coriander leaves
a few slices of **red chilli**

Place the fish on a deep plate slightly larger than
the fish. Use a plate that will fit on the rack of a
traditional bamboo steamer basket or on a steamer
rack inside a wok. Sprinkle the fish with the ginger,
mushrooms, bacon, spring onions, preserved plums,
soy sauce and pepper.

Fill a wok or steamer pan with water, cover and
bring to a rolling boil on a high heat. Set the rack
or basket over the boiling water. Cover and steam
for 15–20 minutes (depending on the variety and
size of the fish) or until a skewer will slide easily
into the fish.

Remove the fish from the steamer and place on
a warm serving plate. Garnish with coriander leaves
and chilli slices, and serve with Jasmine Rice (see
page 126).

For steamed fish with ginger & spring onions, omit
the mushrooms, smoked bacon and preserved plums.
Add 1 tablespoon sunflower oil and 1 tablespoon
sesame oil, and increase the amount of light soy
sauce to 2–3 tablespoons. Drizzle these on top of
the fish with the ginger and spring onions, and steam
as above.

cracked crabs with chillies

Serves **4**

Preparation time **15 minutes**

Cooking time **15 minutes**

500 g (1 lb) live, fresh or
  frozen **crabs**
1½–2 tablespoons **sunflower
  oil**
2–3 tablespoons **Yellow
  Curry Paste** (see page 88)
1 **red onion**, thinly sliced
175 ml (6 fl oz) **coconut milk**
1 large **egg**, lightly beaten
1½–2 tablespoons **fish sauce**
2 **spring onions**, cut into
  2.5 cm (1 inch) lengths

Prepare the crabs (see page 12).

Heat the oil in a wok or large frying pan and stir-fry
the curry paste over a medium heat for 3–4 minutes
or until fragrant.

Add the crab and onion and stir-fry for 7–8 minutes
or until the crab meat is cooked. Add the coconut milk,
egg, fish sauce and spring onions and continue stir-
frying for 2–3 minutes. Taste and adjust the seasoning.

Spoon on to a warm serving plate.

For cracked crab curry, omit the yellow curry
paste and fish sauce. Stir-fry 3–4 finely chopped
garlic cloves with 2 teaspoons curry powder and the
onion until the garlic is lightly browned. Add the crab
and stir-fry for 4–5 minutes. Add the coconut milk,
1 tablespoon light soy sauce, ½ tablespoon oyster
sauce and egg and cook for another 5–7 minutes
or until the crab meat is cooked through and the
sauce is reduced by half. Add the spring onions
and finish as above.

baked fish with lemon grass

Serves **4**

Preparation time **10 minutes**

Cooking time **20–25 minutes**

1 kg (2 lb) **whole fish** (such
as mackerel, St Peter fish,
sea bream, red snapper or
grey mullet), cleaned and
scaled (if necessary), gutted,
scored 3–4 times with a
sharp knife

4 x 12 cm (5 inch) stalks
lemon grass, cut diagonally
into 2.5 cm (1 inch) lengths

2 **carrots**, cut into matchsticks

4 tablespoons **light soy
sauce**

2 tablespoons **lime juice**

1 **red chilli**, finely chopped

To garnish

coriander leaves

a few slices of **red chilli**

a few slices of **lemon**, to serve

Place the fish in a baking dish and sprinkle with the
lemon grass, carrots, 1½ tablespoons of the light soy
sauce and the lime juice.

Cover the baking dish with foil and bake in a
preheated oven, 180°C (350°F), Gas Mark 4, for
20–25 minutes or until a skewer will slide easily into
the flesh and come out clean. Place each fish on a
warm serving plate and spoon over the sauce. Garnish
with coriander leaves and chilli and serve with the
lemon slices.

Spoon the remaining light soy sauce into a small bowl
with the chilli and serve separately.

Serve with other dishes, with boiled rice or on its own
as a light meal with stir-fried or steamed vegetables.

For coley fillets with lemon grass, replace
the whole fish with 4 x 250 g (8 oz) coley fillets,
remove any fine bones. Sprinkle as above and bake
for 15–17 minutes or until the fish is cooked. Garnish
with finely chopped red chilli and serve as above.

clams with ginger

Serves **4** (with 3 other main dishes)

Preparation time **10 minutes**

Cooking time **8–10 minutes**

1 kg (2 lb) **clams** (in their shells)

2 tablespoons **sunflower oil**

4–5 **garlic cloves**, finely chopped

4 tablespoons **vegetable stock**, **seafood stock** or **water**

50 g (2 oz) fresh **root ginger**, peeled, finely sliced

1 tablespoon **oyster sauce**

1–1½ tablespoons **light soy sauce**

2 **spring onions**, finely sliced

coriander leaves, to garnish

Prepare the clams by scrubbing well with a stiff brush under cold running water. Discard any with broken or open shells.

Heat the oil in a wok or large frying pan and stir-fry the garlic over a medium heat until it is lightly browned.

Add the clams and stir-fry over a medium heat for 4–5 minutes. Add the stock or water, ginger, oyster sauce, soy sauce and spring onions and stir-fry for another 2–3 minutes or until all the clams have opened. Discard any shells that have not opened.

Spoon on to a serving plate, garnish with coriander leaves and serve immediately.

For spicy clams with Thai basil, add 1 thinly sliced medium onion and 2–3 lightly bruised bird's-eye chillies to the wok after the garlic has browned. Stir-fry for 2 minutes, then stir in the clams and continue cooking as above. At the end of the cooking time add a handful of Thai basil leaves (omitting the coriander) and toss together before serving.

panaeng fish curry

Serves **4**
Preparation time **10 minutes**
Cooking time **about**
  15 minutes

1½ tablespoons **sunflower oil**
2–3 tablespoons **Dry Curry**
  Paste (see page 194)
300 ml (½ pint) **coconut milk**
1½ tablespoons **fish sauce**
25 g (1 oz) **coconut, palm**
  or **brown sugar,** or
  2 tablespoons **clear honey**
4 **fish fillets** each 250 g
  (8 oz) cod, haddock or sea
  bass, fine bones removed
3 tablespoons **Tamarind**
  Purée (see page 90) or
  2½ tablespoons **lime juice**

To garnish
4 **kaffir lime leaves,** finely
  shredded
a few slices of **red chilli**

Heat the oil in a wok or saucepan. Stir-fry the curry paste over a medium heat for 3–4 minutes or until fragrant.

Add the coconut milk, fish sauce and sugar or honey and simmer gently for 2–3 minutes or until the sugar has dissolved.

Add the fish fillets and the tamarind purée or lime juice. Splash the sauce over the top and cook for 4–5 minutes or until the fish is done, moving it occasionally. The sauce should be slightly mild, sweet and sour to taste, not too hot. Taste and adjust the seasoning.

Spoon on to 4 warm serving plates and garnish with kaffir lime leaves and chilli slices.

For panaeng curry with fish balls, mix 500 g (1 lb) minced fish fillet with 2 tablespoons plain flour. Shape the fish paste into small balls or discs, about 2.5 cm (1 inch) across, with your wet hands. Lower them into the coconut milk after the sugar has dissolved and simmer over a medium heat for 7–8 minutes or until cooked. Continue as above.

deep-fried fish & 3-flavour sauce

Serves **4**
Preparation time **15 minutes**
Cooking time **50 minutes**

7–8 **red chillies**, about
    12 cm (5 inches) long,
    deseeded, chopped
6 **garlic cloves**, roughly
    chopped
8 **shallots**, roughly chopped
5 **coriander roots** and **stalks**,
    roughly chopped
sunflower oil, for deep-frying
150 g (5 oz) **coconut**,
    palm or **brown sugar**, or
    10 tablespoons **clear honey**
3½–4 tablespoons **fish sauce**
5–6 tablespoons **Tamarind**
    Purée (see page 90) or
    5–6 tablespoons **lime juice**
1 kg (2 lb) **whole fish** (such
    as St Peter fish, sea bream,
    red snapper or grey mullet),
    cleaned and scaled (if
    necessary), gutted, scored
    with a sharp knife,
    3–4 times, dried
6 tablespoons **plain flour**

To garnish
coriander leaves
a few slices of **red chilli**

Use a pestle and mortar or small blender to pound or
blend the fresh chillies, garlic, shallots and coriander
roots, forming a rough paste.

Heat 1½ tablespoons of the oil in a wok or large frying
pan and stir-fry the chilli paste over a medium heat for
3–4 minutes until fragrant. Add the sugar or honey,
fish sauce, tamarind purée or lime juice and simmer for
3–4 minutes or until the sugar has dissolved. Taste and
adjust the seasoning. Remove from the heat.

Dust the fish with the flour.

Heat 10 cm (4 inches) of oil in a large wok over a
medium heat. The oil is ready when a piece of garlic
sizzles immediately when dropped in. Deep-fry the fish
on one side for 10–12 minutes or until lightly browned.
Drain on kitchen paper and keep warm. Deep-fry the
remaining fish. Put the fish on a serving plate.

Spoon the warm chilli sauce over the fish and garnish
with coriander leaves and chilli slices.

For deep-fried bean curd with 3-flavour sauce,
replace the fish with 500 g (1 lb) bean curd (tofu), cut
into 1 cm (½ inch) cubes, and deep-fry until lightly
browned but with the inside still soft. Replace the fish
sauce with 3½–4 tablespoons light soy sauce.

salmon with ginger & white fungus

Serves **4**

Preparation time **10 minutes**

Cooking time **15–17 minutes**

handful of **dried white fungus**

4 x 250 g (8 oz) **salmon fillets**

2 **carrots**, cut into matchsticks

5 cm (2 inch) piece of **fresh root ginger**, peeled, finely shredded

20 **sun-dried goji berries** (optional)

¼ teaspoon **ground black pepper**

3 tablespoons **light soy sauce**

4 whole **coriander plants**

4 handfuls of **watercress**, cleaned, shaken dry, to serve

Soak the dried fungus in boiling-hot water for 3–4 minutes, or until soft, then drain. Remove and discard the hard stalks and roughly chop.

Place the salmon fillets on a baking dish and sprinkle with the carrots, ginger, goji berries (if using), pepper, 1 tablespoon of the soy sauce and the fungus. Snap each coriander plant in half and place one on top of each fillet. Cover with foil and bake in a preheated oven, 180°C (350°F), Gas Mark 4, for 15–17 minutes or until a skewer will slide easily into the flesh and come out clean.

Remove the coriander plants. Place a fish fillet with some of the sauce on each warm serving plate. Pile a handful of watercress next to it. Serve the remaining light soy sauce separately in a small bowl. Alternatively, place each fish over boiled rice or cooked noodles, or serve with a vegetable dish such as stir-fried vegetables.

For haddock with ginger & lemon grass, omit the dried white fungus. Use 4 x 250 g (8 oz) fillets of haddock with 4 lemon grass stalks, about 12 cm (5 inches) long, bruised with a rolling pin and cut in half diagonally. Add 2 tablespoons lime juice, drizzle and bake as above.

thai prawn omelette

Serves **4**
Preparation time **10 minutes**
Cooking time **8–10 minutes**

3 **garlic cloves**, roughly
chopped
2 **coriander roots** and **stalks**,
roughly chopped
2 **shallots**, roughly chopped
4 **kaffir lime leaves**, finely
chopped
4 large **eggs**
¼ teaspoon **ground black
pepper**
5 tablespoons **vegetable
stock** or **water**
1 tablespoon **light soy sauce**
125 g (4 oz) **minced prawns**
2 tablespoons **sunflower oil**

Use a pestle and mortar or small blender to pound or
blend the garlic, coriander roots and stalks, shallots and
kaffir lime leaves into a paste.

Beat the eggs, pepper, stock or water, soy sauce and
minced prawns together.

Heat 1½ tablespoons of the oil in a wok or large frying
pan and stir-fry the garlic paste over a medium heat for
2–3 minutes until fragrant. Pour in the egg mixture and
cook for 3–4 minutes. Slide a spatula under the wet
omelette and lift it up in several places around the pan
to let the egg liquid flow on the hot surface so that it
cooks underneath (add more oil if necessary). Flip it
over and continue to cook and brown the other side.

Transfer the omelette to a warm serving plate. Serve
with stir-fried vegetables or curry, and boiled rice.

For egg pancake with red pepper & ginger, omit
the coriander and kaffir lime leaves. Beat the eggs,
shallots, pepper, stock, ½ tablespoon light soy sauce
and minced prawns together. Make the omelette as
above. Heat another tablespoon of oil, ½ tablespoon
sesame oil and lightly brown the finely chopped
garlic. Add 1 thinly sliced red pepper, 75 g (3 oz)
drained and sliced water chestnuts, 1 cm (½ inch)
piece of fresh root ginger, peeled and shredded, and
1 tablespoon light soy sauce. Stir-fry for 3–4 minutes.
Return the omelette pieces to the pan with a handful
of baby spinach leaves. Toss together until the
omelette warms up and the spinach starts to wilt.
Sprinkle with 1 tablespoon toasted sesame seeds
before serving.

seafood with chillies

Serves **4**

Preparation time **5 minutes**

Cooking time **about
10 minutes**

1½ tablespoons **sunflower oil**

3–4 **garlic cloves**, finely
chopped

125 g (4 oz) **red pepper**,
deseeded and cut into bite-
sized pieces

1 **small onion**, cut into
eighths

1 **carrot**, cut into matchsticks

450 g (14½ oz) **prepared
mixed seafood**, such as
prawns, squid, small scallops

2.5 cm (1 inch) piece of **fresh
root ginger**, peeled and
finely shredded

2 tablespoons **vegetable** or
seafood stock

1 tablespoon **oyster sauce**

½ tablespoon **light soy sauce**

1 **long red chilli**, stemmed,
deseeded and sliced
diagonally

1–2 **spring onions**, finely
sliced

Heat the oil in a nonstick wok or frying pan and
stir-fry the garlic over medium heat until it is lightly
browned.

Add the red pepper, onion and carrot and stir-fry for
2 minutes.

Add all the seafood together with the ginger,
stock, oyster sauce and soy sauce and stir-fry for
2–3 minutes or until the prawns turn pink and all the
seafood is cooked.

Add the chilli and spring onions and mix well together.
Spoon on to a serving plate and serve immediately.

For seafood with pineapple sweet chilli, stir-fry
the red pepper, onion and carrot after the garlic has
lightly browned. Add all the seafood, ginger, stock,
oyster sauce and 2–3 tablespoons pineapple-
flavoured sweet chilli sauce (or plain if the flavoured
version is unavailable). Omit the spring onion and add
a handful of Thai basil leaves with the chilli, lightly toss
together for a minute to combine before serving.

green curry with fish

Serves **4**
Preparation time **15 minutes**
Cooking time **10–15 minutes**

1 ½ tablespoons **sunflower oil**
2–3 tablespoons **Green Curry Paste** (see page 200)
400 ml (14 fl oz) can **coconut milk**
50 ml (2 fl oz) **vegetable stock** or **water**
2 ½ tablespoons **fish sauce**
25 g (1 oz) **coconut, palm** or **brown sugar**, or
2 tablespoons **clear honey**
500 g (1 lb) **fish fillets** (such as cod, haddock or halibut), fine bones removed, cut into 3.5 cm (1 ½ inch) pieces
150 g (5 oz) can **water chestnuts**, drained, sliced
4 **cherry tomatoes**, with calix left on if possible
2–3 **kaffir lime leaves**, torn in half

To garnish
Thai sweet basil leaves
a few slices of **red chilli**

Heat the oil in a wok or saucepan and stir-fry the green curry paste over a medium heat for 3–4 minutes or until fragrant.

Add the coconut milk, stock or water, fish sauce and sugar or honey. Simmer over a medium heat for 3–4 minutes or until the sugar has dissolved. Add the fish and the water chestnuts and cook for another 4–5 minutes. Stir gently a few times during cooking. Taste and adjust the seasoning.

Add the tomatoes and kaffir lime leaves in the last few seconds, taking care not to let the tomatoes lose their shape.

Spoon into 4 serving bowls and garnish with basil leaves and chilli slices.

For green curry with mixed vegetables, replace the fish with 300 g (10 oz) pumpkin, sweet potato and marrow, peeled, diced and cooked. Use 2 ½ tablespoons light soy sauce (instead of the fish sauce) and vegetable stock. Add 250 g (8 oz) of sliced courgettes, baby sweetcorn and green beans after the sugar has dissolved and cook for 3–4 minutes. Add the cooked vegetables, warm through and continue as above.

curried seafood in peppers

Serves **4**
Preparation time **30 minutes**
Cooking time **15–18 minutes**

400 ml (14 fl oz) can **coconut milk** (reserve 4 tablespoons)
2–3 tablespoons **Red Curry Paste** (see page 94)
2 large **eggs**
2½ tablespoons **fish sauce**
300 g (10 oz) **mixed seafood** (such as small raw prawns, cod or haddock, cut into 1 cm/½ inch pieces, mussels without shells, small scallops and squid rings)
8 big **romano peppers**
handful of **Thai sweet basil leaves**, **spinach leaves** or shredded **cabbage**
½ teaspoon **plain flour**

To garnish
2 **kaffir lime leaves**, finely shredded
a few slices of **red chilli**

Mix the coconut milk, curry paste, eggs, fish sauce and seafood together in a bowl. Half-fill a wok or steamer pan with water, cover and bring to the boil over a medium heat.

Cut out a long sliver, about 1 cm (½ inch) width, from each of the romano peppers. Remove the seeds and membrane from each 'case', then clean and dry them. Place a few basil or spinach leaves or some shredded cabbage in the bottom of each pepper case. Spoon the seafood mixture into each pepper, almost to the top. Place on a plate that fits in a bamboo steamer basket or on a steamer rack inside the wok. Cover and steam for 15–18 minutes.

Meanwhile, mix the flour and reserved coconut milk in a small saucepan until smooth. Stir and cook over a medium heat for 2–3 minutes or until thick. Spoon a little of it on top of the peppers. Garnish with kaffir lime leaves and chilli slices and serve with boiled rice or cooked noodles.

For curried aubergine with protein mince, replace the seafood with 250 g (8 oz) long purple or green aubergine cut into 1 cm (½ inch) cubes. Toss with ½ teaspoon salt, leave for 30 minutes then squeeze the water out. Soak 50 g (2 oz) dried soya protein mince in hot water for 6–7 minutes, then squeeze the water out. Mix the coconut milk, curry paste, 3 large eggs and 2½ tablespoons light soy sauce. Divide the aubergine and protein mince between individual bowls. Spoon over with the curry sauce mixture, each three-quarters full, and steam as above. Spoon over coconut milk and garnish as above.

prawns with lemon grass & chilli

Serves **4–6**
Preparation time **30 minutes**
Cooking time **20 minutes**

3 x 12 cm (5 inch) stalks
  lemon grass, finely sliced
3–4 **red chillies**, about
  12 cm (5 inches) long,
  deseeded, roughly chopped
6 **garlic cloves**, roughly
  chopped
15 **shallots**, 5 roughly
  chopped, 10 finely sliced
3 **coriander roots** and **stalks**,
  roughly chopped
750 g (1½ lb) medium-sized
  raw **prawns**
sunflower oil, for deep-frying
160 g (5½ oz) **coconut**,
  palm or **brown sugar**, or
  165 ml (5½ fl oz) **clear
  honey**
3½ tablespoons **fish sauce**
5 tablespoons **Tamarind
  Purée** (see page 90) or
  4 tablespoons **lime juice**

To garnish
coriander leaves
a few slices of **red chilli**

Use a pestle and mortar or a small blender to pound or blend the lemon grass, chillies, garlic, chopped shallots and coriander roots and stalks to form a rough paste. Prepare the prawns (see page 13).

Heat 7 cm (3 inches) of oil in a wok over a medium heat. It is ready when a slice of shallot sizzles immediately when dropped in. Deep-fry the sliced shallots for 6–8 minutes until golden brown. Drain on kitchen paper.

Deep-fry the prawns in batches for 3–4 minutes, then drain on kitchen paper.

Remove most of the oil, leaving 1½ tablespoons in the wok. Stir-fry the lemon grass and chilli paste over a medium heat for 3–4 minutes or until fragrant. Add the sugar or honey, fish sauce and tamarind purée or lime juice and cook for 3–4 minutes or until the sugar has dissolved. Add all the prawns and gently toss with the sauce. Taste and adjust the seasoning.

Spoon on to warm serving plates and garnish with coriander leaves and chilli slices.

For prawns with crispy shallots & ginger, deep-fry 10 finely sliced shallots in the oil until golden brown, drain. Use 1½ tablespoons of oil to brown 2–3 finely chopped garlic cloves. Add 2 small carrots, cut into matchsticks, and stir-fry for 2–3 minutes. Add 125 g (4 oz) fresh root ginger, peeled and finely shredded, the prawns, 2 tablespoons oyster sauce, 2 tablespoons light soy sauce, 4 tablespoons water and stir for another 3–4 minutes. Serve garnished with crispy shallots, coriander and chilli.

one-meal
dishes

thai fried noodles with seafood

Serves **4**

Preparation time **20 minutes**

Cooking time **25 minutes**

500 (1 lb) **mixed seafood**

300 g (10 oz) **dried rice noodles**

4½–5 tablespoons **sunflower oil**

3–4 **garlic cloves**, finely chopped

4 large **eggs**

2 **carrots**, cut into matchsticks

4–5 tablespoons **fish sauce**

3½ tablespoons **tomato ketchup**

5 tablespoons **Tamarind Purée** (see page 90) or **lime juice**

1 tablespoon **caster sugar**

¼ teaspoon **chilli powder**

4 tablespoons **preserved turnip**, finely chopped

3–4 tablespoons **ground dried shrimp**

6 tablespoons **roasted peanuts**, roughly chopped

300 g (10 oz) **bean sprouts**

2–3 **spring onions**, cut into 2.5 cm (1 inch) pieces

slices of **red chilli**, to garnish

Prepare the seafood (see page 13).

Cook the noodles in boiling water for 8–10 minutes or according to the packet instructions. Drain, add to a bowl of water until they cool down, then drain again.

Heat 1½ tablespoons of the oil in a wok or large frying pan and stir-fry the garlic over a medium heat for 1–2 minutes or until lightly browned. Add the seafood and cook for 3–4 minutes or until cooked. Remove and set aside.

Add another 1½ tablespoons of oil to the wok. Add the eggs and stir to scramble for 2–3 minutes. Add the remaining oil, noodles and carrots and stir-fry for 3–4 minutes. Add the fish sauce, tomato ketchup, tamarind purée or lime juice, sugar, chilli powder, preserved turnip, dried shrimp and seafood. Add half the peanuts and bean sprouts and all the spring onions. Toss together. Taste and adjust the seasoning.

Spoon on to a serving plate and sprinkle the remaining peanuts over the top. Garnish with coriander leaves and chilli slices. Serve with some lime slices and the remaining bean sprouts.

For vegetarian Thai fried noodles, replace the mixed seafood with 500 g (1 lb) firm bean curd (tofu) cut into 1 cm (½ inch) pieces. Add to the wok after the garlic has lightly browned and stir-fry for 3–4 minutes. Remove and set aside before continuing to cook as above. Omit the fish sauce and dried shrimp and replace with 4½–5 tablespoons light soy sauce.

northern curry with chicken

Serves **4**

Preparation time **15 minutes**

Cooking time **about 30 minutes**

sunflower oil, for deep-frying and stir-frying

125 g (4 oz) **shallots**, finely sliced

300 g (10 oz) **egg noodles**

2–3 tablespoons **Red Curry Paste** (see page 94)

2 teaspoons **ground turmeric**

1 teaspoon **ground cumin**

500 g (1 lb) skinless **chicken fillets**, finely sliced

200 ml (7 fl oz) **coconut milk**

200 ml (7 fl oz) **vegetable** or **chicken stock**

2½ tablespoons **fish sauce**

25 g (1 oz) **coconut, palm** or **brown sugar**, or

2 tablespoons **clear honey**

a few slices of **red chilli**, to garnish

4 **lime slices**, to serve

Heat 7 cm (3 inches) of oil in a wok over a medium heat. The oil must not be too hot. It is ready when a small piece of shallot sizzles immediately when dropped in. Deep-fry the shallots for 6–8 minutes until golden brown. Drain on kitchen paper.

Cook the noodles in boiling water for 8–10 minutes or according to the packet instructions. Keep warm.

Heat 1½ tablespoons of oil in a wok or large frying pan. Stir-fry the curry paste with the turmeric and cumin over a medium heat for 3–4 minutes or until fragrant.

Add the chicken and stir-fry for 4–5 minutes. Add the coconut milk and stock, fish sauce and sugar or honey, then simmer for 3–4 minutes or until the sugar has dissolved, stirring occasionally. Taste and adjust the seasoning.

Divide the noodles between 4 serving bowls. Spoon over the curried chicken and garnish with the chilli slices and crispy shallots. Put a slice of lime at the side of each bowl.

For northern curry with mixed seafood, simmer the coconut milk and stock, fish sauce and sugar after the curry paste becomes fragrant. Add 500 g (1 lb) of the seafood of your choice, cook for 3–4 minutes or as you prefer it, then continue as above.

crispy noodles with vegetables

Serves **4**
Preparation time **15 minutes**
Cooking time **15–20 minutes**

500 g (1 lb) **mixed
  vegetables**, (such as
  broccoli, cauliflower florets,
  thinly sliced carrots, baby
  sweetcorn, mangetout, green
  beans, halved mushrooms,
  chopped spring greens)
about 750 ml (1¼ pints)
  sunflower oil, for deep-
  frying
125 g (4 oz) dried **egg
  noodles**
3–4 **garlic cloves**, chopped
125 g (4 oz) **bean sprouts**
1 cm (½ inch) piece of **fresh
  root ginger**, peeled, finely
  shredded
200 ml (7 fl oz) **vegetable
  stock** or **water**
2 tablespoons **light soy
  sauce**
3½–4 tablespoons **oyster
  sauce**
2 **spring onions**, cut into
  2.5 cm (1 inch) lengths
coriander leaves, to garnish

Blanch the broccoli, cauliflower florets and carrot in
boiling water for 1–1½ minutes. Drain and place in a
bowl of cold water to ensure a crispy texture. Drain
again and place in a bowl with the other vegetables.

Heat 7 cm (3 inches) oil in a wok on medium heat. The
oil is ready when a piece of noodle sizzle immediately
when dropped in. Deep-fry each nest of noodles for
5–6 minutes or until crispy. Drain on kitchen paper and
keep warm.

Pour the oil out of the wok, leaving behind about
1½ tablespoonfuls and stir-fry the garlic on a medium
heat for 1–2 minutes or until lightly browned. Add the
mixed vegetables, bean sprouts and ginger and stir-fry
for another 3–4 minutes. Add the stock, light soy sauce
and 3½ tablespoons oyster sauce and toss together.
Add the spring onions. Taste and adjust the seasoning,
adding the rest of the oyster sauce if necessary.

Arrange the noodles on serving plates and spoon over
the mixed vegetables. Garnish with coriander leaves
and serve.

For crispy noodles with seafood, replace the
mixed vegetables with 500 g (1 lb) of mixed
seafood, such as shelled raw prawns, squid rings,
mussels with shells and small scallops. Lightly
brown the garlic, add 375 g (12 oz) roughly chopped
spring green leaves and stir-fry for 3 minutes. Add
the seafood and bean sprouts and stir-fry for another
3–4 minutes. Finish cooking as above and serve with
the crispy noodles.

spicy noodles with seafood

Serves **4**

Preparation time **15 minutes**

Cooking time **20 minutes**

500 g (1 lb) **mixed seafood**
(such as medium-sized
raw prawns, squid tubes,
mussels without shells and
small scallops)

375 g (12 oz) dried **flat rice
noodles**, about 1 cm
(½ inch) in width

1½–2 tablespoons **sunflower
oil**

3–4 **garlic cloves**, finely
chopped

2–3 small **bird's-eye chillies**,
lightly bruised

2½ tablespoons **fish sauce**

3 tablespoons **seafood stock**
or **water**

handful of **Thai sweet basil
leaves**

Prepare the seafood (see page 13).

Cook the noodles in boiling water for 8–10 minutes or
according to the packet instructions, then drain. Add
water until the noodles cool down, then drain again.

Heat the oil in a wok or large frying pan and stir-fry the
garlic and chillies over a medium heat for 1–2 minutes
or until the garlic has lightly browned. Add the seafood
and stir-fry for 3–4 minutes. Move to the outer edges
of the wok or pan.

Add the noodles, fish sauce and stock or water. Mix
together until the noodles warm through. Add the basil
leaves and stir-fry until the basil begins to wilt. Taste
and adjust the seasoning.

Spoon on to 4 warm serving plates.

For spicy noodles with mixed vegetables, replace
the seafood with 500 g (1 lb) of vegetables such as
broccoli florets, sliced carrots, sliced red peppers,
baby sweetcorn, green beans, mushrooms and
spring green leaves. After the garlic has lightly
browned add the broccoli, carrots and peppers
and stir-fry for 3–4 minutes, then add the sweetcorn,
green beans, mushrooms, spring green leaves and
noodles and continue as above.

stir-fried crabs with noodles

Serves **2–4**
Preparation time **30 minutes**
Cooking time **20 minutes**

1–2 live, fresh or frozen **crabs**
(about 500 g/1 lb total
weight)
125 g (4 oz) **mung bean
vermicelli**
1½–2 tablespoons **sunflower
oil**
2–3 **garlic cloves**, finely
chopped
1 **red onion**, thinly sliced
1 **red pepper**, deseeded, cut
into bite-sized pieces
1 **carrot**, cut into matchsticks
1 cm (½ inch) piece of **fresh
root ginger**, peeled, finely
shredded
1½ tablespoons **light soy
sauce**
1 tablespoon **oyster sauce**

To garnish
coriander leaves
2 **spring onions**, cut into
2.5 cm (1 inch) pieces

Prepare the crabs (see page 12).

Soak the vermicelli in hot water for 4–5 minutes or
until soft. Drain well and cut 4–5 times with a sharp
knife to reduce their length.

Heat the oil in a wok or large frying pan and stir-fry
the garlic over a medium heat for 1–2 minutes or until
lightly browned. Add the crab pieces and stir-fry for
10–12 minutes. Add the onion, pepper and carrot and
stir-fry for 3–4 minutes. Add the noodles, ginger, soy
sauce and oyster sauce and stir-fry for another minute.
Taste and adjust the seasoning.

Spoon on to warm serving plates and garnish with
coriander and spring onions.

For stir-fried crab, vegetables & lily flowers, soak
10 dried lily flowers in boiling water for 8–10 minutes,
drain, and tie a knot in the middle of each one.
Replace the noodles with 400 g (13 oz) mixed
vegetables such as whole small button mushrooms,
sugarsnap peas, green beans or sweetcorns, celery
sticks and carrots sliced into matchsticks. After the
crabs are half cooked, add the mixed vegetables,
lily flowers, red onion, pepper, ginger, 2 tablespoons
light soy sauce and 2 tablespoons oyster sauce and
continue stir-frying for another 6–7 minutes.

noodles with beans & white fungus

Serves **4**
Preparation time **20 minutes**
Cooking time **25 minutes**

75 g (3 oz) **soya protein
    mince**
handful of **dried white fungus**
2 tablespoons **white and
    black sesame seeds**
300 g (10 oz) dried **flat
    rice noodles**
3 tablespoons **sunflower oil**
3–4 **garlic cloves**, chopped
250 g (8 oz) can ready-to-eat
    mixed beans, drained
3 **eggs**
2 **carrots**, cut into matchsticks
150 g (5 oz) **white radish**,
    peeled, cut into matchsticks
4½ tablespoons **light soy
    sauce**
3½ tablespoons **tomato
    ketchup**
1½ tablespoons **caster sugar**
3 tablespoons **lime juice**
3 tablespoons **preserved
    turnip**, finely chopped
¼–½ teaspoon **chilli powder**
150 g (5 oz) **bean sprouts**
coriander leaves, to garnish
slices of **red chilli**, to garnish

Soak the soya protein mince in hot water for 4–5
minutes until soft, then squeeze out the liquid. Soak the
dried fungus in boiling-hot water for 3–4 minutes until
soft, then drain. Discard the hard stalks and chop.

Dry-fry the sesame seeds in a pan over a medium heat
for 3–4 minutes or until lightly browned or popping.
Spoon into a small bowl.

Cook the noodles in boiling water for 8–10 minutes or
according to the packet instructions. Drain, add water
until they cool, then drain again.

Heat 1½ tablespoons of the oil in a wok and stir-fry the
garlic over a medium heat for 1–2 minutes until lightly
browned. Add the protein mince, beans and fungus,
stir-fry for 2–3 minutes, then move to the outer edges
of the wok. Add the remaining oil and scramble the egg
for 2–3 minutes. Add the carrots and white radish and
stir-fry for 3–4 minutes. Add the noodles, soy sauce,
tomato ketchup, sugar, preserved turnip, chilli powder,
bean sprouts and lime juice and stir-fry for another
3–4 minutes. Taste and adjust the seasoning.

Spoon into serving bowls and garnish with the toasted
sesame seeds, coriander leaves and chilli slices.

For noodles with 'flower fireworks', omit the beans
and soya protein mince. Mix 125 g (4 oz) self-raising
flour, ⅓ teaspoon baking powder, ¼ teaspoon salt, a
pinch of ground white pepper, 2 crushed garlic cloves,
2 pounded coriander roots and stalks and 125 ml
(4 fl oz) cold water to make a light lumpy batter.
Splash into the hot oil and deep-fry each batch until
crisp, then drain. Add at the end of the recipe above.

egg-fried noodles

Serves **2**
Preparation time **10 minutes**
Cooking time **20 minutes**

175 g (6 oz) **egg noodles**
2–2½ tablespoons **sunflower oil**
2 **garlic cloves**, crushed
1 **onion**, thinly sliced
250 g (8 oz) **chicken fillets** or **pork fillet**, thinly sliced
2 **eggs**
125 g (4 oz) **crab meat** or prepared **squid**
125 g (4 oz) shelled raw **prawns**
1½–2 tablespoons **light soy sauce**
2½–3 tablespoons **oyster sauce**
ground white pepper

To garnish
coriander leaves
lime rind, finely sliced

Cook the noodles in boiling water for 8–10 minutes or according to the packet instructions. Drain, then leave them in a bowl of cold water until they cool down. Drain again and set aside.

Heat half of the oil in a wok or large frying pan. Add the garlic and stir-fry quickly until lightly browned. Add the onion and chicken or pork and stir-fry for 3–4 minutes, then move to the outer edges of the wok.

Add the remaining oil to the wok or pan and scramble the eggs for 2–3 minutes. Add the crab or squid and prawns and stir-fry for 2–3 minutes. Add the cooked noodles, 1½ tablespoons light soy sauce, 2½ tablespoons oyster sauce and pepper, toss together to warm through the noodles. Taste and adjust the seasoning, using the rest of the light soy sauce and oyster sauce if necessary.

Divide into serving bowls and serve garnished with coriander leaves and lime rind.

For chicken egg-fried noodles with greens, omit the squid or crab meat and the prawns. Add 250 g (8 oz) roughly chopped spring green leaves after scrambling the eggs and stir-fry for 3–4 minutes. Add the cooked noodles and a handful of bean sprouts along with the rest of the ingredients. Adjust seasoning to taste and continue cooking as above.

pork crackling with rice

Serves **4–6**

Preparation time **5 minutes**, plus drying and chilling overnight

Cooking time **36–40 minutes**

1 kg (2 lb) **pork belly** (lean, if possible)

1 teaspoon **sea salt**

2 teaspoons **rice wine vinegar**

sunflower oil, for deep-frying

Clean the pork and cut into 4 pieces, pat dry with kitchen paper and allow to dry for 1 hour.

Use a knife to score through the rind with diagonal cuts about 1 cm (½ inch) apart, in a diamond pattern. Prick the rind all over with a folk. Rub the meat with the salt and the rind with the vinegar. Leave at room temperature for 4–5 hours and keep dry overnight in the refrigerator.

Heat 7 cm (3 inches) of oil in a wok over a medium heat. When the oil appears ready to deep-fry, drop a small piece of garlic into it. If it sizzles immediately, the oil is ready. Lower each piece of pork, rind side down, into the oil and deep-fry for 8–10 minutes until lightly browned and crispy. Drain on kitchen paper. Repeat with the remaining pork pieces. Slice into smaller pieces and arrange on top of boiled rice.

Serve with Sweet Chilli Sauce (see page 36) or use as required.

For pork crackling salad, mix ½ quantity of pork crackling cut into bite-sized pieces with 4 shallots and 3 spring onions, finely sliced, 1–2 small bird's-eye red chillies, finely chopped, 3½ tablespoons lime juice and ½ tablespoon fish sauce. Taste and adjust the seasoning. Spoon over the mixed salad leaves and garnish with coriander leaves and chilli slices.

fried rice with prawns & crab

Serves **4**

Preparation time **15 minutes**

Cooking time **6–8 minutes**

250 g (8 oz) **prawns**

3 tablespoons **sunflower oil**

5–6 **garlic cloves**, finely
   chopped

4 **eggs**

1 kg (2 lb) cooked **rice**,
   refrigerated overnight

250 g (8 oz) can **crab meat**,
   drained

2 teaspoons **curry powder**

1½–2 tablespoons **light soy
   sauce**

1 **onion**, sliced

2 **spring onions**, finely sliced

about 8 cooked **crab claws**,
   125 g (4 oz) in total

½ long **red** or **green chilli**,
   stemmed, deseeded, finely
   sliced, to garnish

Prepare the prawns (see page 13).

Heat half the oil in a wok or large frying pan and stir-fry the garlic over a medium heat until it is lightly browned. Add the prawns and stir-fry over a high heat for 1–2 minutes. Move the prawns out to the edges of the wok or pan.

Add the other half of the oil and scramble the eggs for 1–2 minutes.

Add the rice, crab meat, curry powder, 1½ tablespoons light soy sauce and onion and cook, stirring, for 1–2 minutes. Add the spring onions. In the last minutes of cooking add the crab claws. Taste and adjust the seasoning, using the rest of the light soy sauce if necessary.

Spoon on to a serving dish, garnish with the chilli slices and serve immediately.

For spicy fried rice with sweet pepper, after lightly browning the garlic add 1 sweet red pepper, cut into bite-sized pieces, and 1 thinly sliced onion, then stir-fry for 3–4 minutes. Add the prawns and 2 finely chopped long red chillies and continue cooking as above, omitting the crab meat, curry powder and crab claws.

pineapple fried rice with prawns

Serves **2**
Preparation time **25 minutes**
Cooking time **30–35 minutes**

1 **pineapple**, leaves attached
300 g (10 oz) medium-large
    raw **prawns**
3–3½ tablespoons **sunflower
    oil**
1 large **egg**, beaten with a
    pinch of salt
2–3 **garlic cloves**, finely
    chopped
150 g (5 oz) **ham**, chopped
50 g (2 oz) mixed **sweetcorn
    kernels** and **peas**, defrosted
    if frozen
½ **red pepper**, deseeded,
    diced
1 cm (½ inch) piece of **fresh
    root ginger**, peeled, finely
    shredded
25 g (1 oz) **sultanas**
300 (10 oz) cold cooked **rice**
1 tablespoon **light soy sauce**
2 teaspoons **yellow curry
    powder**
25 g (1 oz) **roasted cashew
    nuts**, to garnish

Cut the pineapple in half lengthways. Scoop out the
flesh to leave 2 shells about 1 cm (½ inch) thick. Cut
the flesh into cubes, place half in a bowl and
refrigerate the rest to use another time.

Wrap the pineapple leaves in foil to stop them burning.
Bake the shells on a baking sheet in a preheated oven,
180°C (350°F), Gas Mark 4, for 10–15 minutes to seal
in the juice. Prepare the prawns (see page 13).

Heat 1½ tablespoons of the oil in a wok or large frying
pan over a medium heat. Pour in the egg and swirl
round the pan to form a thin omelette. Flip to brown the
other side. Remove from the pan and allow to cool
slightly. Cut into thin strips.

Heat the remaining oil and stir-fry the garlic over a
medium heat for 1–2 minutes until lightly browned. Add
the prawns, ham, sweetcorn, peas, pepper, ginger and
sultanas. Stir-fry for 3–4 minutes or until the prawns
open and turn pink. Add the rice, soy sauce, curry
powder and the pineapple and toss over a medium heat
for 5–7 minutes. Taste and adjust the seasoning.

Fill the pineapple shells with fried rice. Garnish with the
omelette strips and cashew nuts and serve.

For pumpkin fried rice & beans, replace pineapple
and prawns with 300 g (10 oz) diced cooked pumpkin
and 250 g (8 oz) mixed beans, drained. Omit the
ham, corn, sultanas and curry powder. Brown the
garlic, add the rice, beans, peas, pepper, ginger and
2–2½ tablespoons soy sauce. Cook for 4–5 minutes.
Add pumpkin and warm through.

fried rice with beans & bean curd

Serves **4**

Preparation time **10 minutes**

Cooking time **7 minutes**

about 750 ml (1¼ pints)
  sunflower oil, for deep-
  frying

½ x 250 g (8 oz) block ready-
  fried **bean curd (tofu)**, diced

2 **eggs**

250 g (8 oz) cold cooked **rice**

1½–2 tablespoons **light soy
  sauce**

2 teaspoons **crushed dried
  chillies**

1 teaspoon **fish sauce** or **salt**

125 g (4 oz) **French beans**,
  finely chopped

25 g (1 oz) **crispy mint**, to
  serve (optional)

Heat the oil in a wok and deep-fry the bean curd over a medium heat until golden brown on all sides. Remove from the oil with a slotted spoon, drain on kitchen paper and set aside.

Remove most of the oil from the wok, leaving behind about 2 tablespoonfuls. Heat this oil until hot, then crack the eggs into it, breaking the yolks and stirring them around.

Add the rice, 1½ tablespoons soy sauce, chillies and fish sauce or salt and French beans and stir-fry for 3–4 minutes. Stir in the bean curd and warm through with the rice for another 2–3 minutes.

Turn on to a dish and serve with the crispy mint, if liked.

For crispy mint, as a garnish, heat 2 tablespoons of groundnut oil in a wok until it is hot. Add 25 g (1 oz) fresh mint leaves and 1 small, finely diced, fresh red chilli to the wok and stir-fry for 1 minute until crispy. Remove with a slotted spoon and drain on kitchen paper.

spicy rice with chicken

Serves **4**
Preparation time **10 minutes**
Cooking time **15 minutes**

1½–2 tablespoons **sunflower oil**
3–4 **garlic cloves**, finely chopped
3–4 small **bird's-eye chillies**, lightly bruised
425 g (14 oz) skinless **chicken fillets**, finely sliced
1 **red onion**, thinly sliced
750 g (1½ lb) cooked **Jasmine Rice** (see page 126), refrigerated overnight
2½ tablespoons **fish sauce**
handful of **Thai sweet basil leaves**

Heat the oil in a wok or large frying pan. Stir-fry the garlic and chillies over a medium heat for 1–2 minutes or until the garlic has lightly browned. Add the chicken and onion and stir-fry for 4–5 minutes or until the chicken is cooked.

Add the rice and fish sauce and stir-fry for another 3–4 minutes. Taste and adjust the seasoning. Add the basil leaves and stir-fry until the basil begins to wilt.

Spoon on to 4 warm serving plates.

For rice with sweet chilli prawns, replace the chicken, garlic and small chillies with 425 g (14 oz) prawns and 2–3 tablespoons Sweet Chilli Sauce (see page 36). (Try to get garlic-flavoured sweet chilli sauce if possible.) Stir-fry the prawns for 2–3 minutes, add the sweet chilli sauce and mix together. Remove to the outer edges of the wok or pan. Add the onion, rice and fish sauce and continue as above.

rice soup with fish

Serves **4**

Preparation time **10 minutes**

Cooking time **15 minutes**

1 ½ tablespoons **sunflower oil**

3–4 **garlic cloves**, finely chopped

1.8 litres (3 pints) **vegetable or seafood stock**

30 **sun-dried goji berries** (optional)

375 g (12 oz) cooked **rice**

2 tablespoons **preserved radish**

3 ½ tablespoons **light soy sauce**

375 g (12 oz) skinless **fish fillets**, fine bones removed, cut into 3.5 cm (1 ½ inch) pieces

handful of **Chinese cabbage** or **chard**, roughly chopped

2.5 cm (1 inch) piece of **fresh root ginger**, peeled, finely shredded

To garnish

2 **spring onions**, finely sliced

coriander leaves

pinch of **ground white pepper**

Heat the oil in a small saucepan and stir-fry the garlic over a medium heat for 1–2 minutes or until lightly browned. Spoon into a small serving bowl.

Heat the stock, goji berries (if using), rice (crumbled apart if necessary) and preserved radish in a saucepan over a medium heat for 6–8 minutes. Add the soy sauce, fish, Chinese cabbage and ginger and cook for another 4–5 minutes or until the fish is cooked, stirring gently from time to time. Taste and adjust the seasoning.

Spoon into 4 serving bowls, garnish with spring onions, coriander leaves and pepper. Drizzle with the garlic oil.

For rice soup with squid balls, replace the fish pieces with 375 g (12 oz) minced squid. Mix together with 2 garlic cloves, finely chopped, 2 coriander roots and stalks, finely chopped, 1 tablespoon plain flour and ¼ teaspoon ground white pepper. Shape into small balls and lower them into the stock after the preserved radish has been added. Continue as above.

fried rice with seafood

Serves **4**

Preparation time **30 minutes**

Cooking time **6–8 minutes**

500 g (1 lb) **mixed seafood** (such as raw prawns, scallops, squid and white fish fillet)

3 tablespoons **sunflower oil**

4 **garlic cloves**, finely chopped

1 kg (2 lb) cooked **rice**, refrigerated overnight

2 **onions**, sliced

2.5 cm (1 inch) piece of **fresh root ginger**, peeled, finely sliced

2½–3 tablespoons **light soy sauce**

3 **spring onions**, finely sliced

1 long **red** or **green chilli**, stemmed, deseeded, finely sliced, to garnish

Prepare the seafood (see page 13).

Heat the oil in a wok or large frying pan and stir-fry the garlic over a medium heat until it is lightly browned.

Add the seafood and stir-fry over a high heat for 1–2 minutes. Add the cooked rice, onions, ginger, 2½ tablespoons light soy sauce and stir-fry for 3–4 minutes. Add the spring onions, taste and adjust the seasoning, using the rest of the light soy sauce if necessary.

Spoon on to a serving plate, garnish with the chilli slices and serve immediately.

For rice soup with seafood, after the garlic has lightly browned, add 500 g (1 lb) cooked rice and stir-fry for 3–4 minutes. Add 1.8 litres (3 pints) seafood or vegetable stock. Omit the onion and add the mixed seafood, ginger, light soy sauce, along with 2 tablespoons preserved radish and a handful of white cabbage. Cook for 3–4 minutes before transferring to serving bowls.

fried rice with salmon omelette

Serves **4**
Preparation time **10 minutes**
Cooking time **25–30 minutes**

5 tablespoons **sunflower oil**
2–3 **garlic cloves**, finely
  chopped
1 **red onion**, thinly sliced
1 **carrot**, cut into matchsticks
50 g (2 oz) **peas**, defrosted if
  frozen
500 g (1 lb) cooked **Jasmine
  Rice** (see page 126),
  refrigerated overnight
125 g (4 oz) can **wild salmon**,
  drained, flaked
1 cm (½ inch) piece of **fresh
  root ginger**, peeled, finely
  shredded
1½ tablespoons **light soy
  sauce**
4 large **eggs**
4 tablespoons **vegetable
  stock** or **water**
⅛ teaspoon **ground white
  pepper**
4 **lime slices**, to serve

To garnish
coriander leaves

Heat 1 tablespoon of the oil in a wok or large frying
pan and stir-fry the garlic over a medium heat for
1–2 minutes or until the garlic has lightly browned. Add
the onion, carrot and peas and cook for 3–4 minutes.
Add the rice, salmon, ginger and soy sauce and stir for
another 4–5 minutes. Taste and adjust the seasoning.
Divide into 4 portions and keep warm.

Beat the eggs, stock and pepper in a bowl. Divide into
4 portions.

Heat a nonstick frying pan over a medium heat and
brush with a little oil. Pour in 1 portion of the egg
mixture, and swirl the pan to form a very thin omelette.
Cook for 1–2 minutes or until almost set. Flip and
lightly brown the other side.

Place 1 portion of the fried rice on one half of the
omelette and fold the other side of the omelette over it.
Keep it warm while making the remaining 3 omelettes
in the same way. Place an omelette on each serving
plate. Garnish with coriander leaves and add a slice
of lime to each plate. Serve with salad, steamed or
stir-fried vegetables.

For spicy fried rice with crab omelette, add

1 tablespoon curry paste and stir-fry with the oil
(omitting the garlic). Replace the salmon with a 125 g
(4 oz) can of crab and cook as above. Place 2 cooked
crab craws next to each omelette before serving.

rice curry with mixed vegetables

Serves **4**
Preparation time **15 minutes**
Cooking time **18 minutes**

300 g (10 oz) **mixed
  vegetables** (such as Thai
  aubergines, thin asparagus,
  courgettes, green beans,
  mangetout, mushrooms and
  baby sweetcorn)
1½–2 tablespoons **sunflower
  oil**
1½–2 tablespoons **Red Curry
  Paste** (see page 94)
200 ml (7 fl oz) **coconut milk**
150 g (5 oz) can **shredded
  bamboo shoots in water**,
  drained
2½ tablespoons **light soy
  sauce**
25 g (1 oz) **coconut, palm**
  or **brown sugar**, or
  2 tablespoons **clear honey**
500 g (1 lb) cooked **Jasmine
  Rice** (see page 126),
  refrigerated overnight

To garnish
coriander leaves
a few slices of **red chilli**

Cut the aubergines into quarters and the asparagus
into 5 cm (2 inch) pieces, slice the courgettes, top and
tail the beans and mangetout and cut them diagonally,
and quarter the mushrooms if large.

Heat the oil in a wok or large frying pan and stir-fry the
curry paste over a medium heat for 3–4 minutes or
until fragrant.

Add the aubergines and stir-fry for 3–4 minutes. Add
the coconut milk, all the rest of the mixed vegetables,
the bamboo shoots, soy sauce and sugar or honey and
cook for 5–6 minutes, stirring gently now and again.

Stir in the rice carefully with the vegetables and
warm through for 3–4 minutes. Taste and adjust
the seasoning.

Spoon on to 4 warm serving plates and garnish with
coriander leaves and chilli slices.

For rice curry with mixed beans, replace the mixed
vegetables with 250 g (8 oz) can ready-to-eat mixed
beans in brine, drained. Use green instead of red curry
paste (see page 200). After the paste has become
fragrant, add the coconut milk, bamboo shoots, soy
sauce, sugar or honey and the mixed beans. Cook for
2–3 minutes, add the rice and mix together.

rice with spicy pork & snake beans

Serves **4**

Preparation time **15 minutes**

Cooking time **18 minutes**

1½–2 tablespoons **sunflower oil**

2–3 tablespoons **Red Curry Paste** (see page 94)

375 g (12 oz) **pork fillets**, finely sliced

250 g (8 oz) **snake beans** or **green beans**, cut into 2.5 cm (1 inch) diagonal lengths

15 g (½ oz) **coconut, palm** or **brown sugar**, or 1 tablespoon **clear honey**

750 g (1½ lb) cooked **Jasmine Rice** (see page 126), refrigerated overnight

1½ tablespoons **fish sauce**

3–4 **kaffir lime leaves**, finely shredded, to garnish

Heat the oil in a wok or large frying pan and stir-fry the curry paste over a medium heat for 3–4 minutes or until fragrant.

Add the pork and stir-fry for 4–5 minutes. Add the beans and sugar or honey and stir-fry for another 4–5 minutes.

Add the rice and fish sauce and stir-fry for 3–4 minutes more. Taste and adjust the seasoning.

Spoon on to 4 warm serving plates and garnish with kaffir lime leaves.

For rice with spicy vegetables, replace the pork and snake beans with 625 g (1¼ lb) mixed sugarsnap peas and baby sweetcorn. Omit the fish sauce. After the curry paste has become fragrant, add the sugarsnap peas and sweetcorn and stir-fry for 3–4 minutes. Add the rice and 2–2½ tablespoons light soy sauce and stir-fry for another 3–4 minutes or until the rice has just warmed through.

vegetarian
dishes

stir-fried mushrooms with ginger

Serves **4** (with 2 other main
dishes)
Preparation time **10 minutes**,
plus soaking
Cooking time **7–8 minutes**

small handful of **dried black
fungus**
1 ½ tablespoons **sunflower oil**
3 **garlic cloves**, finely
chopped
500 g (1 lb) **mixed
mushrooms** (such as oyster,
shiitake and button)
1 small **onion**, cut into
6 wedges
3 tablespoons **vegetable
stock** or **water**
2–2 ½ tablespoons **oyster
sauce**
5 cm (2 inch) piece of **fresh
root ginger**, peeled, finely
sliced
2 **spring onions**, slivered
coriander leaves, to garnish

Soak the dried fungus in boiling-hot water for
3–4 minutes until it is soft, then drain. Remove and
discard the hard stalks.

Heat the oil in a wok or large frying pan and stir-fry the
garlic over a medium heat until it is lightly browned.

Cut any large mushrooms in half and remove the
hard stalks. Add the mushrooms, fungus, onion,
stock, 2 tablespoons of oyster sauce and ginger
and stir-fry for another 4–5 minutes. Taste and
adjust the seasoning, using the rest of the oyster
sauce if necessary.

Spoon on to a serving plate, garnish with coriander
leaves and serve immediately.

For spicy mushrooms with water chestnuts,
replace the black fungus with a small amount of
white fungus. After the garlic has lightly browned
add 1 ½–2 tablespoons roasted curry paste and
the onion, then stir fry for 3–4 minutes. Add the
mushrooms and 150 g (5 oz) sliced canned water
chestnuts, then follow the recipe as above, using
an extra ½ tablespoon of light soy sauce.

curried taro & asparagus

Serves **4**
Preparation time **10 minutes**
Cooking time **about
  25 minutes**

500 g (1 lb) **taro**, peeled, cut
  into 1 cm (½ inch) pieces
1½–2 tablespoons **sunflower
  oil**
2–3 tablespoons **Dry Curry
  Paste**
30 **sun-dried goji berries**
  (optional)
150 g (5 oz) thin **asparagus**,
  sliced into 5 cm (2 inch)
  pieces
200 ml (7 fl oz) **coconut milk**
275 ml (9 fl oz) **vegetable
  stock**
2½ tablespoons **light soy
  sauce**
25 g (1 oz) **coconut**, **palm**
  or **brown sugar**, or
  2 tablespoons **clear honey**
4 **cherry tomatoes**, with calix
  left on if possible
2–3 **kaffir lime leaves**, torn in
  half

To garnish
coriander leaves
a few slices of **red chilli**

Cook the taro in a saucepan of boiling water for
8–10 minutes or until tender, then drain.

Heat the oil in a wok or saucepan. Stir-fry the curry
paste and goji berries (if using) over a medium heat
for 3–4 minutes or until fragrant.

Add the asparagus stalks, coconut milk, stock, soy
sauce and sugar or honey and cook for another
2–3 minutes. Add the asparagus tips and cook for
another 2–3 minutes. Add the cooked taro and just
warm through for 1–2 minutes. Add the tomatoes
and kaffir lime leaves in the last minute, taking care
not to let the tomatoes lose their shape. Taste and
adjust the seasoning.

Spoon into 4 serving bowls and garnish with coriander
leaves and chilli slices.

For homemade dry curry paste, stem, deseed and
roughly chop 2–3 dried red chillies and soak them in
hot water for 3–4 minutes, then drain. (If using fresh
chillies do not soak). Pound or blend them with a
12 cm (5 inch) stalk of finely sliced lemon grass, a
2.5 cm (1 inch) piece of scraped and finely sliced
galangal, 4 chopped garlic cloves, 3 chopped
shallots, 3–4 chopped coriander roots and stalks,
3 sliced kaffir lime leaves, 1 teaspoon shrimp paste,
1 teaspoon ground cumin and 1 teaspoon ground
coriander. Continue until the mixture forms a paste.
You can omit the shrimp paste for a vegetarian
version. Use this quantity of dry curry paste to cook
curries that serve 4 people.

mushroom & mangetout stir-fry

Serves **2**
Preparation time **10 minutes**,
   plus soaking
Cooking time **4–5 minutes**

10 dried **shiitake
   mushrooms**
1½ tablespoons **sunflower oil**
2 **garlic cloves**, finely
   chopped
175 g (6 oz) **baby sweetcorn**,
   diagonally sliced
150 g (5 oz) drained canned
   bamboo shoots
175 g (6 oz) **mangetout**,
   topped and tailed
handful of fresh **bean sprouts**
2–2½ tablespoons **light soy
   sauce**
2 tablespoons **vegetable
   stock** or **water**
ground black pepper,
   to taste

Soak the shiitake mushrooms in boiling water for
10 minutes or until soft, then drain and thinly slice.

Heat the oil in a wok and and stir-fry the garlic over a
medium heat until it is lightly browned. Add all the rest
of the ingredients in turn. Stir-fry over a high heat for
2–3 minutes, then turn out on to a serving dish.

Serve immediately.

For mushroom & spring green noodles, replace
the baby sweetcorn, bamboo shoots and mangetout
with 2 small carrots cut into matchsticks, 1 red sweet
pepper, deseeded and cut into thin strips and 300 g
(10 oz) spring green leaves, roughly chopped and
the stalks discarded. Cook 350 g (12 oz) dried
egg noodles in boiling water for 8–10 minutes or
according to the packet instructions, then drain.
Lightly brown the garlic and stir-fry the carrot, red
pepper, spring green leaves and shiitake mushrooms
for 2–3 minutes. Add the noodles, bean sprouts and
2½–3 tablespoons light soy sauce and stir-fry for
another 3–4 minutes or until the noodles have
warmed through.

sweet & sour ginger & bean curd

Serves **4**
Preparation time **15 minutes**
Cooking time **30–40 minutes**

sunflower oil, for deep-frying
300 g (10 oz) **fresh root
  ginger**, peeled, finely
  shredded
500 g (1 lb) firm **bean curd
  (tofu)**, drained, cut into 1 cm
  (½ inch) cubes
2 **garlic cloves**, finely
  chopped
40 g (1½ oz) **coconut**, palm
  or **brown sugar**, or
  3 tablespoons **clear honey**
2 tablespoons **light soy
  sauce**
2 tablespoons **vegetable
  stock** or **water**
3 tablespoons **Tamarind
  Purée** (see page 90) or
  2 tablespoons **lime juice**

Heat 5 cm (2 inches) of oil in a wok over a medium heat. Deep-fry all the ginger without stirring for 6–8 minutes. Move the ginger with a slotted spoon until golden brown, then drain on kitchen paper.

Lower the bean curd cubes into the oil, in batches, and deep-fry for 5–6 minutes until lightly browned and soft inside. Drain on kitchen paper.

Remove most of the oil, leaving 1½ tablespoons in the wok. Stir-fry the garlic over a medium heat for 1–2 minutes or until lightly browned. Add the sugar or honey, soy sauce, stock or water and tamarind purée or lime juice and stir on a low heat until slightly thickened. Taste and adjust the seasoning. Add the bean curd and most of the crispy ginger and mix together.

Spoon into 4 warm serving bowls and garnish with the remainder of the crispy ginger. Serve with a green or red curry.

For caramel mushrooms, replace the bean curd with 500 (1 lb) oyster mushrooms, torn and air-dried for 4–5 hours. Finely slice 50 g (2 oz) shallots. Omit the ginger and tamarind purée or lime juice. Deep-fry the shallots and dried mushrooms separately until crispy. Continue as above, then add the mushrooms and mix with the slightly thick sauce, using ¼ teaspoon ground white pepper. Stir constantly for 4–5 minutes or until quite dry. Sprinkle with crispy shallots before serving.

green curry in soya milk

Serves **4**
Preparation time **15 minutes**
Cooking time **25 minutes**

425 g (14 oz) **mixed hard vegetables** (such as pumpkin, winter squash and marrow) and **mixed soft vegetables** (such as Thai aubergines, baby sweetcorn, courgettes, mushrooms, asparagus and green beans)
1½–2 tablespoons **sunflower oil**
2–3 tablespoons **Green Curry Paste**
25 **sun-dried goji berries** (optional)
475 ml (16 fl oz) **soya milk**
3 tablespoons **light soy sauce**
15 g (½ oz) **coconut**, **palm** or **brown sugar**, or
1 tablespoon **clear honey**
150 g (5 oz) **pineapple** or **pineapple slices in light juice**, cut into pieces

To garnish
Thai sweet basil leaves
a few slices of **red chilli**

Peel and slice the hard vegetables and cut into 2.5 cm (1 inch) cubes. Quarter the aubergines and slice the courgettes and mushrooms. Cut the asparagus into 2.5 cm (1 inch) pieces and top and tail the beans. Cook the hard vegetables in boiling water over a medium heat for 8–10 minutes or until soft, then drain.

Heat the oil in a wok or saucepan. Stir-fry the curry paste and goji berries (if using) over a medium heat for 3–4 minutes until fragrant. Add the aubergines, courgettes and mushrooms and stir-fry for 4–5 minutes. Add the asparagus, sweetcorn and green beans and gently stir-fry for another 2–3 minutes.

Add the soya milk, soy sauce, sugar or honey, cooked hard vegetables and pineapple and warm through for 2–3 minutes, stirring occasionally. Taste and adjust the seasoning.

Spoon into 4 serving bowls and garnish with Thai sweet basil leaves and chilli slices.

For homemade green curry paste, blend 3–4 small green chillies, stemmed, with a 12 cm (5 inch) stalk of finely sliced lemon grass, a 2.5 cm (1 inch) scraped, finely sliced piece of galangal, 2 chopped kaffir lime leaves, 4 chopped garlic cloves, 3 chopped shallots, 3 chopped coriander roots and stalks, a small handful of coriander leaves, a small handful of Thai sweet basil leaves, ¼ teaspoon ground white pepper and a teaspoon each of shrimp paste, ground coriander and ground cumin. Continue until the mixture forms a paste. Use this quantity of green curry paste to cook curries that serve 4 people.

golden bean curd with garlic

Serves **4**

Preparation time **15 minutes**

Cooking time **20–25 minutes**

5–6 **garlic cloves**, roughly chopped

4 **coriander roots** and **stalks**, roughly chopped

20 **black peppercorns**

4 tablespoons **sunflower oil**

500 g (1 lb) firm **bean curd (tofu)**, drained, cut into 2.5 cm (1 inch) cubes, dried

1 **red** or **yellow pepper**, deseeded, cut into bite-sized pieces

1 cm (½ inch) piece of **fresh root ginger**, peeled, finely shredded

1–2 **spring onions**, cut into 2.5 cm (1 inch) lengths

2½ tablespoons **light soy sauce**

To garnish
coriander leaves
a few slices of **red chilli**

Use a pestle and mortar or a small blender to pound or blend the garlic and coriander roots and stalks into a paste. Add the peppercorns and continue to pound roughly.

Heat a little of the oil in a nonstick frying pan and gently pan-fry the bean curd, in batches, making sure there is a slight gap between the cubes. Fry each side for 1–2 minutes until lightly browned. Remove and keep warm. Add a little oil to the pan before cooking each further batch.

Heat the remainder of the oil in a wok or large frying pan and stir-fry the garlic paste over a medium heat for 3–4 minutes or until fragrant.

Add the pepper and stir-fry for 3–4 minutes, then add the bean curd, ginger, spring onions and soy sauce. Gently toss together for another 2–3 minutes. Taste and adjust the seasoning.

Spoon on to a warm serving plate and garnish with coriander leaves and chilli slices. Serve with boiled rice or spoon over noodles.

For mushrooms with water chestnuts & ginger, replace the bean curd with 375 g (12 oz) mixed mushrooms and 75 g (3 oz) canned water chestnuts, drained and sliced. Add to the pan at the same time as the peppers and stir-fry for 5–6 minutes. Add the ginger, spring onions and light soy sauce. Adjust to taste. You may want to add a little bit more light soy sauce.

jungle curry with vegetables

Serves **4**
Preparation time **15 minutes**
Cooking time **20 minutes**

500 g (1 lb) **mixed hard
vegetables** (such as
pumpkin, winter squash and
marrow) and **mixed soft
vegetables** (such as Thai
aubergines, courgettes,
mushrooms, thin asparagus,
baby sweetcorn, green
beans and spring green
leaves)
1.2 litres (2 pints) **vegetable
stock**
2–3 tablespoons **Jungle
Curry Paste**
20–25 **sun-dried goji berries**
(optional)
50 g (2 oz) **lesser ginger
(krachai)**, thinly scraped,
finely shredded
3½ tablespoons **light soy
sauce**
2–3 **kaffir lime leaves**, torn in
half
coriander leaves, to garnish

Peel and slice the pumpkin, winter squash and
marrow and cut into 1 cm (½ inch) cubes. Quarter the
aubergines and slice the courgettes and mushrooms.
Cut the asparagus into 2.5 cm (1 inch) pieces. Top and
tail the green beans and cut diagonally. Roughly chop
the spring green leaves.

Heat the stock with the curry paste and goji berries
(if using) in a saucepan over a medium heat for
2–3 minutes or until boiling. Add the hard vegetables
and cook for 8–10 minutes. Add the aubergines,
courgettes, mushrooms and asparagus and cook for
3–4 minutes. Add the sweetcorn, green beans, spring
greens, lesser ginger and soy sauce and cook for
another 1–2 minutes, stirring occasionally. Taste and
adjust the seasoning.

Spoon into 4 serving bowls and garnish with coriander
leaves. Serve with rice.

For homemade jungle curry paste, pound or blend
3–4 chopped fresh red chillies, stemmed, a 12 cm
(5 inch) stalk of finely sliced lemon grass, a 1 cm
(½ inch) piece of scraped and finely sliced galangal,
4 chopped garlic cloves, 3 chopped shallots and
3–4 chopped coriander roots and stalks. Continue
until the mixture forms a paste.

mixed vegetables & sesame seeds

Serves **4**

Preparation time **15 minutes**

Cooking time **12 minutes**

500 g (1 lb) **mixed
vegetables** (such as baby
carrots, broccoli florets, thin
asparagus, red or yellow
pepper, courgettes, baby
sweetcorn, mangetout, green
beans, mushrooms and
spring green leaves)

1 cm (½ inch) piece of **fresh
root ginger**, peeled, finely
shredded

½ tablespoon **white sesame
seeds**

1½–2 tablespoons **sunflower
oil**

3–4 **garlic cloves**, finely
chopped

125 g (4 oz) **bean sprouts**

2 tablespoons **vegetable
stock** or **water**

2–2½ tablespoons **light soy
sauce**

2 **spring onions**, cut into
2.5 cm (1 inch) lengths

a few **cherry tomatoes**, with
calix left on if possible

coriander leaves, to garnish

Cut the asparagus into 5 cm (2 inch) pieces, keeping
the stems and tips separate. Deseed the pepper and
cut into bite-sized pieces. Slice the courgettes thinly.
Top and tail the mangetout and green beans and cut
diagonally. Roughly chop the spring green leaves.

Blanch the carrots and broccoli florets in boiling water
for 1 minute. Add the asparagus stems and continue
for another minute. Drain and place in a bowl of cold
water for a crispy texture. Drain and combine with all
the other vegetables and ginger.

Dry-fry the sesame seeds in a nonstick frying pan
over a medium heat. Shake the pan to move the
seeds around for 3–4 minutes or until they are lightly
browned and popping. Spoon into a small bowl.

Heat the oil in the same wok and stir-fry the garlic over
a medium heat for 1–2 minutes or until lightly browned.
Add the mixed vegetables and bean sprouts and stir-fry
for 3–4 minutes. Add the stock and soy sauce and toss
together. Add the spring onions and cherry tomatoes in
the last few seconds, making sure the tomatoes don't
lose their shape. Taste and adjust the seasoning.

Spoon on to a serving plate, sprinkle sesame seeds on
top and garnish with coriander leaves.

For chilli mixed vegetables & almonds, replace the
sesame seeds and bean sprouts with 15 g (½ oz)
flaked almonds and 75 g (3 oz) can water chestnuts,
drained and sliced. Pan-fry the almonds for 3–4
minutes or until lightly browned. Add 2 tablespoons
sweet chilli sauce (see page 36) to the pan after soy
sauce and sprinkle over the stir-fry before serving.

pumpkin curry with green beans

Serves **4**
Preparation time **10 minutes**
Cooking time **20 minutes**

500 g (1 lb) **pumpkin,** peeled,
cut into 1 cm (½ inch) cubes
1½–2 tablespoons **sunflower
oil**
2–3 tablespoons **Massaman
Curry Paste** (see page 116)
30 **sun-dried goji berries**
(optional)
1 **onion,** thinly sliced
25 g (1 oz) **roasted peanuts**
50 g (2 oz) **green beans,**
topped and tailed, cut
diagonally
400 ml (14 fl oz) **soya milk,**
well stirred
2½ tablespoons **light soy
sauce**
40 g (1½ oz) **coconut,
palm** or **brown sugar,** or
3 tablespoons **clear honey**
2 tablespoons **lime juice**
2 medium-sized **tomatoes,**
quartered
a few slices of **red chilli,**
to garnish

Cook the pumpkin in a saucepan of boiling water for
8–10 minutes or until tender, then drain.

Heat the oil in a saucepan and stir-fry the curry paste,
goji berries (if using), onions and peanuts over a
medium heat for 3–4 minutes or until fragrant.

Add the green beans and cook for 2–3 minutes. Add
the soya milk, soy sauce, sugar or honey, lime juice and
pumpkin and warm through for 2–3 minutes, or until
the sugar has dissolved, stirring occasionally. Taste and
adjust the seasoning. Add the tomatoes in the last few
seconds.

Spoon into 4 serving bowls and garnish with a few
slices of chilli.

For vegetable curry with water chestnut, replace the
pumpkin with 500 g (1 lb) of a cubed hard vegetable
(such as sweet potato, winter squash, marrow, white
radish or taro). Cook the cubed vegetable until tender
before adding to the curry, as above. Omit the green
beans and replace them with 50 g (2 oz) thinly sliced
canned water chestnut. Continue cooking as above.

mixed vegetable curry & 5-spice

Serves **4**
Preparation time **15 minutes**
Cooking time **17 minutes**

625 g (1¼ lb) **mixed hard
  vegetables** (such as
  pumpkin, sweet potatoes
  and taro)
50 g (2 oz) **mixed soft
  vegetables** (such as baby
  sweetcorn, green beans or
  mangetout)
1½–2 tablespoons **sunflower
  oil**
2–3 tablespoons **Red Curry
  Paste** (see page 94)
2 teaspoons **5-spice powder**
25–50 g (1–2 oz) **roasted
  peanuts**
8 small **shallots**, peeled
200 ml (7 fl oz) **coconut milk**
350 ml (12 fl oz) **vegetable
  stock** or **water**
2½ tablespoons **light soy
  sauce**
40 g (1½ oz) **coconut, palm**
  or **brown sugar**, or
  3 tablespoons **clear honey**
2 tablespoons **lime juice**
4 **cherry tomatoes**
a few slices of **red chilli**, to
  garnish

Peel and cut the hard vegetables into 1 cm (½ inch)
cubes. Cut baby sweetcorn in half diagonally and top
and tail green beans or mangetout.

Heat the oil in a wok or saucepan and stir-fry the
curry paste, 5-spice powder, peanuts and shallots
over a medium heat for 3–4 minutes or until fragrant.

Add the coconut milk, stock, hard vegetables, soy
sauce and sugar or honey and cook for 8–10 minutes
or until tender, stirring occasionally. Add the soft
vegetables and lime juice and cook for another
2–3 minutes. Taste and adjust the seasoning. Add
the tomatoes in the last few seconds, taking care
not to let the tomatoes lose their shape.

Spoon into 4 serving bowls and garnish with
chilli slices.

For bean curd curry & 5-spice, replace the
mixed vegetables with firm bean curd (tofu), cut into
1 cm (½ inch) cubes. After the curry paste becomes
fragrant, add the coconut milk, stock, soy sauce,
sugar or honey and soft vegetables and cook for
2–3 minutes. Add the lime juice and bean curd,
warm through for another 2–3 minutes and continue
as above.

stuffed omelette

Serves **1**
Preparation time **8–10 minutes**, plus soaking
Cooking time **8–10 minutes**

2½ tablespoons **sunflower oil**
2 **garlic cloves**, chopped
1 **shallot**, finely chopped
4 chopped **French beans**
2 chopped **asparagus**
3 **baby sweetcorn**, thinly sliced
1 **tomato**, diced
4 dried **shiitake mushrooms**, soaked, drained, sliced
2 teaspoons **light soy sauce**
1 **egg**, beaten with a pinch of salt and pepper
crispy basil, to garnish (optional)

Heat 1 tablespoon of the oil in a wok, add the garlic and shallot and stir-fry for 1–2 minutes or until the garlic has lightly browned. Add the beans, asparagus, sweetcorn, tomato, mushrooms and soy sauce and stir-fry for another 3–4 minutes. Remove the filling from the wok and set aside. Wipe the wok clean with kitchen paper.

Pour the remaining oil into the wok and heat it, making sure the oil coats not only the base of the wok but as much of the sides as possible. Pour off any excess. Pour in the eggs, swirling them around to form a large, thin omelette. Make sure it is not sticking to the wok, adding a little more oil if necessary.

Put the filling in the middle when the omelette is almost firm and fold both sides and ends over to form an oblong parcel, constantly ensuring that the omelette is not sticking underneath.

Remove the omelette from the wok carefully and place it in a serving dish. Garnish with crispy basil, if liked, and serve immediately.

For crispy basil, to use as a garnish, heat 2 tablespoons of groundnut oil in a wok until it is hot. Add 25 g (1 oz) of fresh Thai basil leaves and 1 small, finely diced, fresh red chilli to the wok and stir-fry for 1 minute until crispy. Remove with a slotted spoon and drain on kitchen paper.

desserts

flaky pearls & black kidney beans

Makes **20**

Preparation time **1½ hours**

Cooking time **25–30 minutes**

375 g (12 oz) can **black
    kidney beans**, drained

300 g (10 oz) **caster sugar**

4 tablespoons **sunflower oil**

2 **egg yolks**, lightly beaten,
    for brushing

Pastry A

250 g (8 oz) **self-raising flour**

1 tablespoon **caster sugar**

¼ teaspoon **sea salt**

6 tablespoons **sunflower oil**

100 ml (3½ fl oz) **water**

Pastry B

150 g (5 oz) **self-raising flour**

5 tablespoons **sunflower oil**,
    plus extra for brushing
    baking sheet

2 tablespoons **water**

Use a blender to process the beans to a smooth paste.
Stir the paste, sugar and oil in a saucepan over a
medium heat for 10–15 minutes to form a ball. Allow
to cool, then roll into 20 small balls.

Make pastry A. Mix the flour, sugar and salt in a
bowl. Make a well and add the oil. Gradually add the
measured water and knead to a smooth dough. Make
into 10 balls and cover with clingfilm.

Make pastry B. Lightly mix the flour and oil in a bowl.
Gradually add the measured water and knead until it
holds together. Make into 10 balls and cover with
clingfilm.

Take a ball of pastry A and flatten it to make a disc.
Wrap a ball of pastry B with the disc, then squeeze
together. Roll out a rectangle. Take the short edge and
roll tightly into a tube. Flatten the pastry lengthways to
form a rectangle. Repeat. Roll into a tube and cut in
half. Take one half and turn it vertically so it rests on
the cut section, then roll it into a round thin sheet.
Place a black bean ball in the middle. Press the edges
together to seal and place on a lightly oiled baking
sheet, sealed side down. Repeat with the remaining
pastry and filling until you have 20.

Brush each flaky pearl with egg yolk and bake in a
preheated oven, 180°C (350°F), Gas Mark 4, for
25–30 minutes. Serve hot or warm.

sticky rice with mango

Serves **4**

Preparation time **10 minutes**,
  plus soaking and resting

Cooking time **22–28 minutes**

250 g (8 oz) **white sticky rice**

100 ml (3½ fl oz) **coconut milk**

50 ml (2 fl oz) **water**

75 g (3 oz) **palm** or **coconut sugar**

¼ teaspoon **salt**

4 ripe **mangoes**

Coconut cream topping (optional)

100 ml (3½ fl oz) **coconut milk**

½ teaspoon **plain flour**

a pinch of **salt**

Soak the rice in a bowl of water for 3 hours. Drain then spread the rice in a steamer basket lined with muslin.

Fill a wok or a steamer pan with water and bring to the boil. Set the steamer over the water and steam on a medium heat for 20–25 minutes or until the rice swells.

Mix the coconut milk, measured water and sugar and salt in a small saucepan until smooth.

Spoon the hot rice into a bowl and mix it with the coconut milk mixture. Cover and leave to rest for 10 minutes.

Mix the coconut milk, flour and salt together for the coconut cream topping and gently heat in a saucepan for 2–3 minutes.

Peel the mangoes, cut into small slices and arrange on each plate. Serve with the sticky rice and drizzle with the topping, if liked.

For jack fruit (*khanun*) & sticky rice, replace the mango with 25–30 ripe jack fruit pulps. Cut the top end of each and remove seeds and any brown skin they leave behind. Use a teaspoon to fill the insides of the jack fruit pulps with steamed sticky rice with coconut milk. Serve at room temperature with coconut ice cream.

coconut custard

Serves **4**

Preparation time **10 minutes**,
   plus dissolving the sugar

Cooking time **10–15 minutes**

150 ml (¼ pint) **coconut milk**

75 g (3 oz) **coconut**, **palm**
   or **brown sugar**, or
   5 tablespoons **clear honey**

2 large **eggs**

¼ teaspoon **sea salt**

1 teaspoon **vanilla extract**

Make the custard by mixing together the coconut milk, sugar or honey, eggs, salt and vanilla extract and setting aside until the sugar has dissolved. (You can do this a few hours in advance or overnight to make sure all the sugar dissolves completely.)

Half-fill a wok or a steamer pan with water, cover, and bring to a rolling boil over a high heat.

Meanwhile, strain the custard through a sieve into a jug. Pour into individual bowls or ramekins until each is three-quarters full (or use a shallow baking dish that fits inside the steamer).

Place the custard bowls inside the steamer basket or rack. Cover, reduce the heat to medium and cook for 10–15 minutes (increase the cooking time if using a baking dish). Serve at room temperature or chilled.

For coconut custard with lemon grass, bruise and roughly slice 2 lemon grass stalks. Mix and squeeze with 200 ml (7 fl oz) coconut milk, 100 g (3½ oz) sugar and all the other ingredients to release the perfume. Discard the lemon grass when you strain the custard.

banana fritters

Serves **4**

Preparation time **8 minutes**

Cooking time **10 minutes**

sunflower oil, for deep-frying

4–5 **bananas** or 14–15 small **plantains**

caster sugar, to serve

Batter

125 g (4 oz) **self-raising flour**

1 teaspoon **baking powder**

2 teaspoons **sugar**

¼ teaspoon **salt**

25 g (1 oz) freshly grated or desiccated **coconut**

175 ml (6 fl oz) **water**

Make the batter by mixing the flour, baking powder, sugar, salt and coconut in a bowl. Add the measured water and mix it with a fork or spoon until smooth.

Heat 7 cm (3 inches) of oil in a nonstick wok over a medium heat. While it is heating, peel the bananas or plantains, cut each banana into half lengthways, then cut them into 5 cm (2 inch) slices. Halve the plantains lengthways and then slice each length in half. The oil is ready when a little batter sizzles when dropped in.

Coat the banana slices with the batter and then lower them carefully into the hot oil, 6–7 pieces at a time. Cook the bananas over a medium heat for 6–7 minutes until golden brown. Remove the fritters from the oil with a slotted spoon and drain on kitchen paper.

When all the slices are cooked, arrange them on a serving dish and serve at once, sprinkled with sugar, if liked.

For sweet potato & sesame fritters, replace the banana with 750 g (1½ lb) of sweet potato. Cut the sweet potato into slices of roughly 1 x 10 cm (½ x 4 inches). Add 2 tablespoons of sesame seeds to the batter mixture. Dip the sweet potato into the batter and deep-fry for 5–6 minutes. Check they are done by breaking one in half, if it is soft inside then they are cooked.

lemon grass & coconut ice cream

Serves **4–5**
Preparation time **10 minutes**,
   plus infusing and freezing
Cooking time **15 minutes**

3 x 12 cm (5 inch) stalks
   lemon grass, bruised,
   roughly sliced
200 ml (7 fl oz) **coconut milk**
200 ml (7 fl oz) **double cream**
1 large **egg**
2 **egg yolks**
125 g (4 oz) **caster** or **fine
   brown sugar**
pinch of **sea salt**

Mix the lemon grass with the coconut milk, squeezing it to release the perfume. Leave to infuse for 30 minutes. Squeeze once more, strain and then discard the lemon grass.

Fill a wok or large saucepan with water and bring to the boil over a medium heat. Meanwhile, put the lemon grass and coconut milk mixture in a saucepan with the double cream, stir over a gentle heat without boiling for 3–4 minutes and set aside.

Place the egg, egg yolks, sugar and salt in a large heatproof bowl over the boiling water. Use an electric mixer to whisk the mixture for 3–4 minutes until frothy and thickened. Gradually add the lemon grass and coconut milk mixture and mix for another 5–6 minutes to make a thin cream. Leave to cool, pour into a plastic container and freeze for 3 hours or until half-frozen.

Take the ice cream out and 'comb' it with a fork once or twice during the freezing time. Cover and freeze completely. Remove the ice cream from the freezer at least 10–15 minutes before serving so that it becomes slightly softened. Serve on its own or with White Sticky Rice (see page 220).

For ice cream with sweet basil seeds, make the ice cream as above and freeze for 3 hours or until half-frozen. Add ½ tablespoon sweet basil seeds to a bowl of 150 ml (5 fl oz) water. The seeds will expand within a minute or so. Stir to separate and add to the ice cream, mix together and place back in the freezer. 'Comb' once or twice during the freezing time.

coconut balls

Makes **12**
Preparation time **15 minutes**,
   plus cooling and setting
Cooking time **20 minutes**

250 g (8 oz) grated **fresh
   coconut**, or **desiccated
   coconut** softened with a
   little cold water
300 g (10 oz) **sugar**
300 ml (½ pint) **water**

Mix the coconut, sugar and measured water together in a saucepan and then stir on a low heat until the syrup has almost all evaporated.

Put 12 tablespoonfuls of the mixture on a metal baking sheet lined with greaseproof paper, shaping each spoonful into a ball as you go.

Allow to cool for about 1 hour to harden the outside a little, leaving the insides soft.

For sticky coconut sauce, follow the method as above, adding an extra ⅛ teaspoon salt and cooking over a low heat until a sticky caramel sauce has formed. Do not let it thicken to a point where it will harden. Use this sauce over black sticky rice or steamed sticky rice with coconut milk.

watermelon sorbet

Serves **4–6**

Preparation time **10 minutes**,
  plus freezing

1.5 kg (3 lb) **sweet red
  watermelon flesh**,
  deseeded
juice of **1 orange**
rind of ½ **orange**
1 cm (½ inch) piece of **fresh
  root ginger**, peeled and
  finely sliced

Chop the watermelon into cubes and place with the orange juice, orange rind and ginger in a food processor. Process for 1–2 minutes until smooth.

Pour the mixture into a freezer box and freeze for 1½ hours or until half-frozen. Take the mixture out of the freezer and whisk again in a food processor. Return to the container. Whisk at least twice more during the freezing time. There should be plenty of air whipped into the sorbet or it will be too icy and hard. Cover and freeze completely.

For cantaloupe & lychee sorbet, replace the watermelon with 1 ripe medium-size cantaloupe, peeled, deseeded and cut into 2.5 cm (1 inch) pieces. Replace the orange juice and zest with juice and zest from half a lime. Process the cantaloupe in a mixer for 2–3 minutes or until smooth. Add the flesh from 550 g (1 lb 4 oz) canned lychees (reserve the syrup) and give a few more pulses, then pour the mixture into a bowl. Warm the lychee syrup with 1 cm (½ inch) piece of fresh root ginger, finely grated, for 2–3 minutes. Allow to cool before adding it to the cantaloupe and lychee mixture. Whisk twice during freezing.

banana in coconut cream

Serves **4**

Preparation time **10 minutes**

Cooking time **10 minutes**

400 ml (14 fl oz) can **coconut milk**

125 ml (4 fl oz) **water**

50 g (2 oz) **caster sugar** or 4 tablespoons **clear honey**

5 just-ripe **bananas**

½ teaspoon **sea salt**

Heat the coconut milk, measured water and sugar or honey together in a saucepan over a medium heat for 3–4 minutes.

Peel the bananas and cut into 5 cm (2 inch) lengths. If using very small bananas, leave them whole.

Add the bananas and salt to the pan. Cook on a low–medium heat for 4–5 minutes or until the bananas are soft.

Divide the banana and coconut cream between 4 serving bowls and serve warm or at room temperature.

For pumpkin in coconut cream, replace the bananas with 375 g (12 oz) of pumpkin, peeled, cut into matchsticks and soaked in water with a little lime juice (this will help to stop them from darkening). Heat the coconut milk and 200 ml (7 fl oz) water. Add the pumpkin and cook for 8–10 minutes or until tender. Add the sugar and salt and cook until the sugar has dissolved.

black sticky rice & egg custard

Serves **4**

Preparation time **10 minutes**, plus soaking and setting

Cooking time **about 50 minutes**

250 g (8 oz) **black sticky rice**

100 ml (3½ fl oz) **coconut milk**

50 ml (2 fl oz) **water**

75 g (3 oz) **palm** or **coconut sugar**

Custard

75 ml (3 fl oz) **coconut milk**

5 large **eggs**

250 g (8 oz) **coconut** or **palm sugar**, cut into small pieces if hard

1 teaspoon **vanilla extract**

Soak the rice in a bowl of water for at least 3 hours or overnight.

Make the custard. Mix together the coconut milk, eggs, sugar and vanilla extract until the sugar has dissolved. Pour the custard through a sieve into a steamer bowl until it is three-quarters full. Taking care not to burn your hand, set the custard bowl inside the steamer basket or rack, simmer for 10–15 minutes, until set around the edges, and set aside. Leave to set at room temperature for about 30 minutes.

Drain and spread the rice into the same steamer basket over a double thickness of muslin. Cover and simmer for 30–35 minutes or until the rice swells and is glistening and tender. Check and replenish the water every 10 minutes or so.

Mix together the coconut milk, measured water and sugar and set aside until the sugar has dissolved.

Spoon the rice into a bowl as soon as it is cooked. Mix in the coconut milk mixture, cover and set aside for 10 minutes. Serve the black sticky rice on a small dessert plate and spoon the custard over the top.

index

acknowledgements

Executive editor: Nicola Hill
Editor: Ruth Wiseall
Executive art editor: Sally Bond
Designer: Geoff Borin
Photographer: Eleanor Skan
Home economist: Annie Rigg
Props stylist: Liz Hippisley
Production controller: Carolin Stransky

Special photography: © Octopus Publishing Group Limited/Eleanor Skan
Other photography: © Octopus Publishing Group Limited/David Loftus 4, 47, 91, 99, 117, 129; /Neil Mersh 109, 113, 169; /Sandra Lane 23, 27, 37, 43, 65, 83, 87, 103, 119, 147, 161, 177, 199, 215, 221, 225, 229; /William Reavell 21, 79, 95, 125, 137, 173, 183, 195, 235.